Pivot to Succe

Transforming Marketing

Missteps into Milestones

ISBN-13: 9798992897807

Cover design by: Vicky Wu

Printed in the United States of America

Dedication

To the countless entrepreneurs navigating the dizzying world of digital marketing: this book is for you. Especially if you feel like something that someone told you was wrong.

Born from a desire to cut through the noise and offer you genuine, practical advice with no bullshit, I hope it can serve you as a beacon in the often-overwhelming sea of marketing misinformation.

To my husband. When you asked what I had been typing away at for so long, I said "a book". You asked, "how long have you been writing a book?" I answered, "30 years." Your belief in my dreams means the world to me. Thank you for being my sounding board, and for the countless cups of coffee you delivered to my desk that fueled this journey.

To my sons, who made me a mom and have always filled my life with pride, laughter, and endless love. To your wonderful partners and our adorable grandkids – you are the joy that brightens every day and my reason for everything.

To my extended family, who have stood together through life's highs and lows. Your support, especially in recent times of loss, has been a source of immense strength.

And lastly, to my clients, who have entrusted me with the lifeblood of their businesses – your marketing. Your faith in me has been the greatest honor of my professional life.

This book is a piece of my life, a collection of lessons learned, and a testament to the power of resilience, humor, and love. May it guide you, inspire you, and remind you that you're never alone on this journey.

Table of Contents

Introduction

Welcome to a journey of transformation, where the **missteps of marketing** can turn into the **steppingstones to success**. I'm Vicky Wu, and over the past three decades, I've navigated the tumultuous waters of marketing, helping businesses not just to sail but to soar. One of my favorite things in my career is not reaching goals but exceeding them! I've brought that same competitive nature to the goals of tens of thousands of entrepreneurs that I've helped. And now I want to share my expertise with you.

I will be sharing examples of some of the **most common marketing mistakes entrepreneurs make**, and help you pivot from those mistakes to marketing which is designed to help you generate sales.

This book isn't just a collection of strategies; *it's a testament to the power of marketing done right*—marketing that's as unique as the businesses and entrepreneurs it serves.

My passion for marketing sparked as a young artist. Those early days of creativity and imagination have fueled my approach to marketing, blending art with science, intuition with strategy, data with psychology, and vision with execution. From Fortune 500 companies to the vibrant heart of small businesses, I've honed my skills and crafted a marketing philosophy that's as effective as it is distinctive.

But why write this book for you? Over my decades of marketing experience, I've worked with Fortune 500 companies, multi-million and multi-billion-dollar organizations and seen the vast resources they have at their fingertips. An entire floor or more of the corporate headquarters just for marketing, and a guy whose job is nothing but running a report? Wouldn't that kind of team make running a business easy!

I've also seen too many entrepreneurs *lost in the marketing maze*, equipped with tools that don't fit their needs and have them trying to *pound a huge square peg into a small round hole*, following advice that leads them astray. I've witnessed the frustration of **wasted time and resources**, and I've felt the deep satisfaction of helping these entrepreneurs turn it all around.

So now I bring all of that marketing knowledge to the entrepreneurs who would not otherwise have access to the level of expertise that those guys with really deep pockets have access to. This book lets you pick my brain.

Through these pages, I'll guide you to **see beyond the one-size-fits-all solutions that don't work** long-term, and help you recognize the unique marketing blueprint that already lies within your business.

You'll hear **stories of real entrepreneurs**—some which may reflect your own journey—whose missteps I've helped transform into milestones. From the professional who thought they could do it all, to the visionary who was misled by fleeting trends, their stories are woven into the fabric of this book, providing both cautionary tales and triumphant victories.

As we embark on this journey together, you'll discover that your business is a living, breathing entity with *its own identity, goals, and path to success*. And your marketing should be a reflection of that uniqueness. I bring to you the best practices from the giants of industry, distilled and tailored for the entrepreneur, the small business, the dreamers, and the doers.

So, whether you're a seasoned business owner or just starting to realize your dream, this book is for you. It's for those who are ready to pivot from confusion to clarity, from frustration to fulfillment, and from missteps to milestones.

No marketing bullshit here. Just solid advice and an informative journey.

Let's turn the page and begin.

Part I: Recognizing the Missteps

In the first leg of our journey, we'll start to navigate the labyrinth that is the marketing world. It's a place where many entrepreneurs, armed with ambition and drive, find themselves wandering, often veering off into murky waters.

This section is about recognizing those moments when you've taken a wrong turn and understanding that every entrepreneur's journey through the marketing maze is unique.

The Marketing Maze

Marketing is not a straight line; it's a complex maze with many turns, dead ends, and hidden passages. It's easy to feel lost, to run in circles, chasing tactics that end up leading nowhere.

Here, we'll dissect this maze, highlighting the common pitfalls that trap unwary entrepreneurs. You'll learn how to spot the signs that you're stuck in a loop and how to find your way out. Through a case study of an entrepreneur who once was lost in this very maze, we'll explore the transformative moment when they found the right path, with a little guidance and a new perspective.

The One-Size-Fits-All Fallacy

The market is flooded with cookie-cutter solutions, promising success to anyone who uses them. But the truth is, there's no universal key to marketing success. If there were, no business - no matter the size - would ever really need marketing at all!

In this section, we debunk the myth of the one-size-fits-all approach. You'll see how a business can outgrow its initial marketing strategies and why it's essential to evolve. A case study will highlight a company that thrived once it shed the ill-fitting strategies it had learned and embraced a bespoke marketing plan.

The DIY Dilemma

The do-it-yourself route is a rite of passage for many entrepreneurs. It's a testament to the spirit of independence and resilience that defines the entrepreneurial mindset.

But there comes a time when DIY marketing becomes a roadblock to growth. I'll share experiences with DIY marketing—the successes, the failures, and the insights gained. This anecdote will set the stage for understanding when and why to seek professional help, and how it can turn your marketing from a solo struggle into a symphony of collaborative success.

Here in Part I, you'll find the courage to find where you've gone astray and the wisdom to chart a new course.

What's in it for you? Clarity, confidence, and the first steps toward a marketing strategy that's as effective and unique as your business deserves. Let's peel back the layers of confusion and start the transformation.

The Marketing Maze

Welcome to the labyrinth of modern marketing, where every turn could lead to a **breakthrough** or a **dead end**. I've spent over three decades helping entrepreneurs navigate this maze, and not just to find their way, but to discover shortcuts to success that others might miss. This isn't about following a single thread through the labyrinth; it's about understanding the maze itself, mastering its twists and turns, and emerging victorious.

In this section, we'll dissect the **overwhelming world of marketing advice**. You'll learn to sift through the noise, to distinguish between the advice that's merely loud and the guidance that's actually clear.

We'll start with the Google Dilemma, where a simple search can lead to a billion voices shouting for attention, each claiming to have the secret to your success. But as we'll see, the first piece of advice you hear isn't always the one you need.

We'll explore the **perils of generic advice**, where one-size-fits-all tips fall short of addressing the unique challenges your business may face. You'll understand why the most popular strategies aren't always the most profitable and why the path of least resistance can sometimes lead to the greatest struggles.

The Social Media Trap is next, where 'experts' abound, each with a strategy that's worked for them but may not work for you. We'll discover the risks of following a single path and the importance of a strategy that evolves with your business. We'll see the pitfalls of confusing social media activity with effective marketing.

Then, we'll examine **AI and the future of search**, where algorithms shape the landscape of advice which you receive. You'll learn about the limitations of AI in understanding the subtleties of your business and the strategies that will drive it forward. We'll discuss the battle for the top spot in search results and why any website being first in search results doesn't always mean having the best advice for your business.

Finally, we'll talk about the need for personalized guidance. In a world awash with generic advice, the true value lies in strategies tailored to your business's unique challenges and goals. You'll learn to **determine when you need professional expertise** in cutting through the clutter, helping you to not just hear, but listen; to not just follow, but lead.

As we conclude this section, we'll summarize the key points and reinforce the importance of discerning, personalized marketing strategies. I'll invite you to critically evaluate the marketing advice you encounter and to embrace the benefits of expertise that's as unique as your business. But first, let's reflect.

Marketing Mirror

What are the top three unique qualities of your business that set you apart from your competitors?

_____

_____

Describe your target customer. What specific needs of this customer does your business uniquely fulfill?

_____

_____

The Google Dilemma

Imagine this: you're an entrepreneur and you've just typed "small business marketing" into Google's search bar.

In less than a second, the screen floods with results—***over a billion results*** (per Google, "about 1,130,000,000").

Holy cannoli, Batman!

It's like dying of thirst and needing one quick drink of water to sustain you, and instead someone opens the valve on a firehose with so much water coming at you, so fast, that you can't get a single drop.

This is the Google Dilemma, where the *abundance of information* becomes the very thing that *stifles your progress*. (Keep in mind, I'm writing this just before Google's AI search has been released to everyone but while I've been beta testing it … this new technology changes things, and not necessarily in a good way for you accessing the best information. I'll get to that in a bit.)

Back to your billion results - at least how they look in 2023 and the beginning of 2024. The first few links, tagged with 'Ad', promise quick solutions and services. They're the low-hanging fruit of the search results, but sometimes, **they come with a cost that isn't just monetary**. They may offer a piece of the puzzle, but rarely the whole picture, and they're vying for your click, your time, and your wallet.

Scroll past the ads, and you encounter the first organic result. It's a listicle, something like: "10 Small Business Marketing Strategies That Work." At a glance of the title and snippet, it seems helpful, but dig slightly deeper, and you'll find it's a **surface-level rehash of the same old tactics**— email marketing, social media presence, maybe a nod to SEO … blah blah blah. (I'm betting it's the most basic of basics that you already know). It's not that this advice is bad; it's just that it's the marketing equivalent of a beginner's guide to sticking a toe in the kiddie pool when you're needing to dive in the deep end.

Then there are the social media "gurus[1]," each with a sponsored post claiming they've cracked the code.

They'll teach you their 'revolutionary' method, but here's the catch: **it's a one-trick pony.** It worked for them, in their specific context, with their particular audience, and now they're selling it as a panacea. And in some cases, they're selling that process to others to teach you—it's like they're all part of a "**marketing MLM**[2]", which is great for them, but

---

1 My business name used to be "Vicky Wu Marketing Guru" which is what my assistant at my last CMO position called me. It rhymed and had a good flow. A year in, I realized how many self-proclaimed "gurus" actually didn't know what the hell they were talking about and dropped that word from my business name.

2 We've all heard of MLMs but this isn't your grandma's Tupperware party. I use "marketing MLM" to define marketers who teach people their marketing system - the only system they know with only one way of doing things - and then those people have others pay to teach them the one system - and so on, and so on - and pretty soon 99% of the people offering "marketing" services are just selling this same one way to do it. They just slap their own name on it. We're not hobbits … there's more than one ring.

maybe not for you. Your business isn't a carbon copy of theirs; your market, your products, and your customers are as unique as your business.

How do you identify them? Sometimes it's as simple as them talking about how much money their business makes; you need to keep in mind that what worked for them may not be right for you (assuming, of course, that they're not just flat out lying).

This is the crux of the Google Dilemma. The sheer volume of results is overwhelming, and the quality is wildly inconsistent.

The top search results are not necessarily there because they're the best for you—it may only be because *they're the best at playing the SEO game.* They've mastered *the art of ranking high*, not necessarily the art of **delivering value**. While some may have the perfect advice for you, if you're not already an expert at what you need, it can be hard to separate the wheat from the chaff.

And this is where the real challenge lies.

It's not just about finding marketing advice; *it's about finding the right marketing advice for your business at this point in its journey*. It's about discerning which strategies

---

will serve your long-term goals and which are merely distractions. Which you can build upon so that they will serve you both now and in the future.

A wrong approach is to blindly follow the first piece of advice or the most popular strategies without considering their relevance to your unique business needs.

So, how do you navigate this digital deluge? How do you sift through a billion pieces of advice to find the nuggets of wisdom that will truly make a difference for your business?

The answer lies in a combination of *critical thinking* plus *professional guidance*. It's about learning to look beyond the first page of search results, to question the validity of the advice you're given, and to seek out strategies that are tailored to your business's unique needs and goals.

But I also realize that you may not have time to undertake this level of deep research. Most of the phenomenally successful entrepreneurs that I know do not.

In the following sections, we'll explore how to do that but **in a way that makes it efficient**. We'll delve into the perils of generic advice, the pitfalls of following a single path, and the importance of personalized guidance. We'll equip you with the tools to cut through the noise and find the clarity your business deserves.

Let's move beyond the Google Dilemma and into a space where the advice you receive is as specific and as strategic as the business you're building.

The Social Media Trap

Social media platforms have become the town squares of the internet—a place where ideas are shared, voices are heard (sometimes whether you want to hear them or not), and personalities shine. It's no wonder that the rise of the self-proclaimed 'Expert' has been meteoric in this space. These self-proclaimed gurus often come with compelling stories of success, screenshots of impressive metrics, and a one-size-fits-all strategy that they assure will work for everyone.

But herein lies the trap in what can become the social media cesspool.

The Rise of the 'Expert'

The internet is teeming with individuals who have found one strategy that worked wonders for them. They package this strategy, polish it with testimonials, and present it as **the golden ticket to marketing success**.

Or maybe they're at the stage still *hoping* this method will work, since they learned it from someone else who said it will, and they're at the "fake it 'til you make it" stage.

What's often missing from their narratives is the **context**—the unique combination of timing, audience, and market conditions that played a crucial role in their success. Without this context, replicating their results is not just difficult; it's often unrealistic.

In some cases, *using the word expert is a stretch*. I can't tell you how many people I see who have done a bit of social media marketing for one month, for one *free* client, and then proclaim to others that they're an expert for hire. See also: **Fakexpert**[3].

These are often the same people who think social media IS marketing, when in reality it's one tiny tactic of one small piece of marketing. (Visit my blog and search for the 5 Ps of Marketing: product, place, price, promotion, people. You'll see social media doesn't even make the main list.)

The wrong way to use social media is to equate *social media activity* with *effective marketing* and to rely on a single strategy that worked for someone else. Many, many entrepreneurs fall into this trap, so if you have, you're not alone.

The correct approach is to use social media as *one tool* in a comprehensive marketing strategy, focusing on metrics that

---

3 A portmanteau of 'fake' and 'expert', this term is reserved for those who talk the talk but couldn't walk the walk if they had a map and someone to carry them. They're often spotted sporting a library of buzzwords but lacking in the library of results.

align with actual business growth, like conversion rates and customer loyalty.

The Risk of Following a Single Path

Adopting a single, untested path in marketing is akin to navigating a complex network of roads with a map and not a single one has a clear destination. It's restrictive and risky. A strategy that isn't versatile enough to adapt to the changing landscape of your business and market is a strategy that will soon become *obsolete*.

For instance, consider the engagement numbers I found on some famous Facebook pages. I study these regularly from very well-known names in different fields. In the case of well-known marketers I've researched, some of these have training they will sell you and tell you all about how to get engagement from social media ... yet *they aren't getting their own*.

A deep dive into the data reveals a shocking truth: even the most 'successful' pages often have engagement rates at 0.01% or lower (that's less than one tenth of one percent). If you only have 10,000 followers and only get one tenth of one percent engagement ... that's *one* person.

And social media response is only getting worse since the date I did my last study.

Social media is not marketing. It's a tool—a powerful one, but still just one part of the whole. The confusion arises when social media metrics, the likes, and the shares, are *mistaken for genuine business growth*. It's easy to get caught up in the vanity metrics and lose sight of what truly matters: conversions, customer loyalty, and most importantly revenue.

Expert vs. Novice

The difference between an expert and a novice in marketing can often be distilled down to one word: **strategy**. A true marketing professional understands that strategy is about creating a comprehensive plan that's bespoke to your business's unique needs. It's about directing your efforts towards meaningful goals and measurable success.

Incorporating insights from seasoned professionals can help steer your business towards seven-figure success and beyond. It's about leveraging experience and expertise to craft a marketing approach that's as dynamic and multifaceted as the market itself.

Actionable Insights

So, what can you do to avoid the social media trap? Here are some actionable insights drawn from the resources provided:

- **Look Beyond Vanity Metrics:** Focus on engagement that leads to conversions. Track how your social media efforts translate to actual business growth.

- **Context is Key:** Understand that strategies successful for others may not fit your unique business context. Tailor your approach to your audience and market conditions.
- **Strategy Over Tools:** Use social media as one of many tools in your marketing toolkit. Ensure it's integrated into a broader, strategic marketing plan.
- **Seek Professional Guidance:** Consider consulting with a marketing professional who can provide a holistic view and help you navigate beyond social media to the full spectrum of marketing avenues.
- **Test and Adapt:** Be prepared to test different strategies and adapt based on performance data. What works today may not work tomorrow, so stay agile.

By recognizing the limitations of social media, especially the many risks in relying on it as your primary or only strategy, and the importance of a comprehensive, adaptable marketing strategy, you can avoid the pitfalls that ensnare many entrepreneurs.

It's not about discarding social media but about placing it within a larger, more effective framework that drives real business results.

AI and the Future of Search ... and Everything

As we delve deeper into the digital age, the role of artificial intelligence (AI) in shaping our online experiences becomes increasingly significant. AI algorithms are becoming the unseen architects of our digital journeys, influencing the search results we see and the content we consume.

This technological evolution has profound implications for marketing, particularly in how businesses are discovered and how advice is disseminated.

The Emergence of AI in Search ... and Everywhere!

While most of us are looking excitedly at the prospects that AI can bring us—I've been testing it for over six years already at the time of this writing—we focus on *how it can benefit us*.

But when you're an entrepreneur looking for ways to boost your business, there's aspects of AI that *can be a drawback* which you may not have considered which I wanted to bring to your attention.

AI is revolutionizing search engines, transforming them from simple query-based tools to sophisticated platforms capable of understanding and predicting user intent. These algorithms analyze vast amounts of data, learning from user interactions to refine and personalize search results.

26

For marketers, this means that the visibility of their advice and strategies is increasingly subject to the whims of AI. **The strategies that surface at the top of search results** are often there because *they're what the AI thinks you want to see*, **not necessarily *what's most effective* for your unique business**.

The Limitations of AI

Despite its advancements, AI is not infallible. It excels at processing data and identifying patterns but lacks the human capacity to *understand the subtleties and complexities* of individual business needs. (At least, not without a lot of data, which you wouldn't have about marketing strategies used by other businesses to see if it makes sense for your own).

AI can guide a user to content which presents a strategy that is said to have *worked for similar businesses*, but it cannot assess whether that strategy aligns with the unique values, goals, and circumstances of each business.

This limitation means that while AI can offer suggestions, it cannot replace the nuanced advice that comes from a seasoned marketing professional.

The Battle for the Top Spot

Search engine optimization (SEO) has become a battleground where strategies vie for visibility. A well-optimized page may climb to the top of search results, but this placement doesn't guarantee the effectiveness of the strategy it promotes.

The criteria for ranking well—old standbys like keyword usage, backlinks, domain authority—are not the same as those for *a successful marketing strategy*. (And even those are changing). This disconnect can lead businesses to adopt **strategies that look good on paper** (or on the screen) but don't deliver results in the real world.

When we talk about "AI" in the context of searches and content, think of it as a super-smart predictor, like a digital crystal ball. It's not yet actually "intelligent" … not quite the sentient robots from sci-fi movies, but rather a clever program that's really good at guessing what you're going to say next. How? By learning from a vast depository of words and phrases everyone else has used on the internet. It's like having a librarian who's read every book in the world and can predict the next line in any story based on what's been written before. This AI is less about creating innovative ideas and more about being a master of patterns and predictions in language and creating an output for you based upon this.

It's a **language predictor** … and the language it predicts may not always be the language you need right now.

The Disconnection from Results

The ultimate goal of any marketing strategy is to achieve tangible results—increased sales, higher conversion rates, and growth in customer loyalty. However, the metrics used by AI and SEO *to evaluate content* are often disconnected from these business outcomes.

A strategy might be widely shared and cited (remember how I mentioned 'marketing MLM'? Lots of people are citing those strategies!), ticking the boxes for SEO, yet may not translate into actual success for businesses that implement it.

The Challenge of Relevance and Results

The new AI-driven search engines are becoming adept at sifting through content to find topics that match user queries. However, determining the right strategy for a business involves more than matching topics. It requires an understanding of the business's market position, competitive landscape, and internal capabilities—factors that AI is currently unable to assess.

More importantly, AI cannot *verify the results that a particular strategy promises*. It can't tell if the businesses that used a certain tactic saw a real return on their investment or if the strategy is just well-presented.

This gap highlights the need for businesses to look beyond search engine rankings and seek out **strategies with a proven track record of delivering real-world results**.

While AI has transformed the search landscape, it's crucial for entrepreneurs to recognize its limitations. The top search results may not always represent the best advice for your business. As we move forward, the expertise of marketing professionals remains indispensable—providing the context, understanding, and experience that AI cannot replicate. Businesses must critically evaluate the strategies they encounter, looking for evidence of success and alignment with their unique needs, rather than relying solely on the prominence of search engine placement.

The Need for Personalized Guidance

The one-size-fits-all marketing approach is a myth that can often lead businesses astray. The truth is, every business is a unique entity with its own set of challenges, goals, and market dynamics. This uniqueness demands marketing advice that is not just general but bespoke, not just standard but customized.

The Value of Bespoke Strategies

Generic marketing strategies are like **ready-to-wear garments**; they might look good on the model and technically fit you, but they won't complement the unique contours of your business in every case. (Believe me … there are things off the rack that NEVER look right on me. I'm 5'4", but my legs are as long as my husband's, who is 6'! Short torso long legs vs long torso short legs. I can steal his sweats, but his T-shirts fit me like a minidress.)

Bespoke strategies, on the other hand, are the **tailored suits** of the marketing world—they are crafted to fit your business's specific needs, accentuating its strengths and addressing its weaknesses.

These strategies consider your business's unique selling points, target audience, competitive landscape, and long-term objectives among other things. They are designed not just to attract attention, but to convert and retain customers in a way that aligns with your business's core values and vision.

The Role of Professional Expertise

Navigating the ocean of marketing information is daunting. Without a compass, it's easy to drift off course. Professional marketing guidance serves as that compass, offering **direction and clarity** amidst the cacophony of advice. A seasoned marketing professional brings to the table years of experience, a wealth of knowledge, and a toolkit of strategies that have been tested and proven across various industries and market conditions.

They can help you cut through the noise, identify the tactics that will work for your business, and adapt them as your business evolves.

Cutting Through the Noise

As we conclude this exploration of the marketing maze, the key takeaway is clear: **discernment is crucial**. In a world where everyone has something to say about marketing, it's essential to filter out the noise and focus on advice that is relevant and personalized to your business.

The right strategy is not the one that's loudest or most popular, but the one that resonates with your business's unique DNA and helps you achieve your specific goals.

As you move forward on this journey, I encourage you to critically evaluate the marketing advice you receive.

Ask yourself:

- Does this strategy align with my business's values? If it's having you do something that doesn't feel aligned with your values, it's time to pass.
- Is it designed to meet my specific objectives? There are a lot of ways that you can get to your objective, but if it appears that you're needing to add a lot of paths, or it talks about a lot of unrelated objectives, it may not be the right fit.
- Can it adapt as my business grows? A strategy that works now but that is hard to adapt or build upon later will only keep you where you currently are.

If the answer is no, it may be time to seek out professional expertise. Remember, there is no substitute for strategies that are as distinctive and dynamic as your business itself. Let's step beyond the generic and embrace the power of personalized marketing guidance.

Marketing Mirror

Reflect on a recent marketing campaign. What were the specific challenges you faced and how did you attempt to address them?

_____

_____

_____

List down the marketing tactics you have tried in the past. Which ones worked, which didn't, and why?

_____

_____

_____

_____

Marketing Mirror Quiz: Are You Using Generic Strategies?

Answer Yes or No to each question by putting a checkmark in the appropriate column. Remember, there are no right or wrong answers, this is simply a self-assessment.

	YES	NO
Have you ever found yourself struggling trying to make something that a vendor did "fit" your business?	☐	☐
Do you often find yourself implementing marketing strategies because they are popular or trending, rather than because they suit your specific business needs?	☐	☐
Have you adopted marketing tactics without customizing them to your target	☐	☐

audience's preferences or
behaviors?

Do you rely heavily on broad, ☐   ☐
non-specific messaging in
your marketing campaigns?

Is your marketing plan more ☐   ☐
reactive (based on
competitors' actions) rather
than proactive and original?

Have you missed performing ☐   ☐
market research in shaping
your marketing strategies?

Do you find that your ☐   ☐
marketing approach does not
strongly reflect your
business's unique values or
identity?

Are you unsure about the specific return on investment (ROI) for your major marketing campaigns? ☐ ☐

Do you struggle to differentiate your brand in your marketing materials from those of your competitors? ☐ ☐

Have you avoided personalizing your marketing messages because it seems too complex or time-consuming? ☐ ☐

Is your marketing strategy more focused on quantity (e.g., number of posts, ads) than on quality and relevance to your audience? ☐ ☐

Scoring:

Give yourself 1 point for every "Yes" answer.

0-3 Points: You're likely employing a fairly personalized approach to marketing.

4-6 Points: There's a mix of generic and customized elements in your marketing. Consider focusing more on strategies tailored to your business.

7-11 Points: Your marketing strategy leans heavily towards generic approaches. You need this book. It's time to pivot towards more strategic options tailored for your unique business.

Key Takeaways

- Navigate the complexities of marketing by identifying common pitfalls and developing strategies to overcome them.

- Understand the overwhelming nature of abundant information and learn to effectively filter and utilize relevant data.

- Be cautious of self-proclaimed marketing 'experts' on social media and understand the need for strategies that are tailored to your specific business needs.

- Recognize the evolving role of AI in shaping digital marketing and adapt your strategies to stay ahead in a technologically advancing landscape.

The One-Size-Fits-All Fallacy

Welcome to the crossroads of marketing individuality, where the well-worn path of universal solutions diverges into the uncharted territory of **bespoke strategies**. This section isn't about adopting a catch-all approach; it's about recognizing and embracing the distinct identity of your business in the vast marketing landscape.

Here, we'll unravel the myth of the universal marketing solution. You'll learn why the seductive promise of a one-size-fits-all strategy is not just ineffective but can be a disservice to the individuality of your business. We'll begin by exploring **the allure of these so-called universal solutions** and why they captivate many entrepreneurs.

We'll delve into a case study that illustrates the pitfalls of applying a generic strategy without aligning it with the business's unique needs. Through this real-life example, you'll witness the transformative power of customizing strategies for growth.

Next, we confront the funnel fallacy, challenging the notions that you don't have a funnel, and that a single type of marketing funnel is sufficient for all. You'll see why the design of your marketing funnel should be as bespoke as the products or services you offer.

I'll present another case study, focusing on a business whose growth trajectory outpaced its initial marketing funnel. This highlights the signs that indicate the need for a strategy overhaul and the establishment of a funnel that truly fits.

As we progress, you'll be guided on how to assess your own marketing needs, with practical steps to identify when a strategy is no longer serving its purpose. We'll discuss the importance of transitioning to a tailored approach, emphasizing flexibility and adaptation as cornerstones of effective marketing planning.

In concluding this section, we'll encapsulate the key takeaways about the dangers of generic solutions and the value of marketing diversity. I'll encourage you to embrace the unique aspects of your business and reflect them in your marketing efforts.

Together, let's step beyond the fallacy of one-size-fits-all and craft a marketing narrative that truly represents the heart and soul of your enterprise.

Exploring Marketing Individuality

In today's bustling marketplace, where businesses clamor for attention, there lies a fundamental truth often overlooked: *each business possesses a unique identity, a DNA that sets it apart from the rest*. This identity is not just a logo or a tagline; it's the **embodiment of values, visions, and the very essence** of what makes a business resonate with its customers.

It's often this individuality that dictates a business's path to success and its connection with its audience.

Yet, in the pursuit of growth, entrepreneurs frequently stumble into the common misstep of *adopting a one-size-fits-all marketing approach*. It's an easy trap to fall into, seduced by the promise of quick fixes and the success stories of others. If only it were that easy! You wouldn't need me ;)

But as I've already mentioned, what works for one may not work for another, and this is where the misalignment begins. Marketing strategies are not interchangeable garments to be swapped at will; they are tailored suits, meticulously crafted to fit the contours of each unique business profile.

The one-size-fits-all approach is akin to forcing a big square peg into a small round hole—it not only fails to leverage the unique strengths of a business but can also obscure its true potential. When marketing strategies are homogenized, they lose the power to speak directly to the hearts and minds of the target audience, diluting the brand's message and diminishing its impact.

Entrepreneurs must recognize that their business's individuality is its greatest asset in marketing.

Individuality is the compass that should guide every campaign, every message, and every customer interaction. By embracing this individuality, marketing becomes not just a tool for sales, but a platform for storytelling, for building relationships, and for creating an enduring brand that stands out in a sea of sameness.

In the following sections, we'll explore the pitfalls of the one-size-fits-all fallacy and the transformative power of marketing individuality. We'll see through case studies and real-world examples how a bespoke approach to marketing not only aligns with the unique identity of a business but also paves the way for authentic and sustainable growth.

Let's continue on this journey and discover and **amplify the unique voice of your business** in the marketplace.

The Myth of the Universal Solution

The allure of universal marketing solutions is undeniable. They promise a straightforward path to success, a blueprint that any business can follow to achieve their goals. Simply do A + B and it = C. (If that actually worked … you wouldn't need someone to help you. Ever. And you wouldn't need me. Or this book.)

Do you know who these templated strategies work best for? *The person selling it to you. Not you.*

This appeal is rooted in our **desire for simplicity and certainty** in an increasingly complex world. The idea that there's a one-size-fits-all strategy out there is comforting, but as we peel back the layers, we find that this is a myth that can lead businesses astray. It's also easy, especially when we are starting out; we don't need to research, we simply copy what others have done.

I always advocate for taking *any* action in marketing – **starting somewhere is better than not starting at all**. However, I also recognize from my own experience that there comes a point, often sooner than expected, where it's crucial to pivot towards more strategic and effective marketing approaches, especially if you want to grow.

In my experience, and as I've passionately outlined in my marketing blogs, the concept of a universal solution in marketing is not just flawed, it's fundamentally **misleading**. It suggests that all businesses, regardless of their industry, audience, or vision, can follow the same roadmap and expect the same results. This ignores the rich tapestry of variables that make each business unique, and the nuanced understanding required to engage with different audiences effectively.

The pitfalls of applying generic marketing strategies are numerous.

For one, they can lead to a *monotonous brand voice* that fails to differentiate your business in the market. When you use the same tactics as everyone else, you blend into the background noise, and your message loses its impact.

Moreover, these strategies often *lack the flexibility to adapt* to the changing needs of your business and its customers. They can become outdated quickly, leaving you with a stagnant marketing approach in a constantly dynamic marketplace.

Another limitation is the *misallocation of resources*. Universal solutions don't (can't) take into account the specific goals and capacities of your business. You may find yourself investing in channels or tactics that don't align with where your audience actually spends their time or makes their purchasing decisions. This can lead to disappointing results and wasted budgets.

In my call to arms against universal marketing solutions, I emphasize the importance of **careful questioning and customization**. It's essential to *question the relevance* of any given strategy to your unique business context. What works for a large e-commerce platform may not work for a local boutique, and what drives engagement in one industry may not translate to another.

The key is to develop a marketing strategy that is as unique as your business. This means taking the time to *understand your audience deeply*, to identify *what sets your brand apart*, and to craft a narrative that *resonates with your customers*. It's about creating a marketing ecosystem that aligns with your business **values**, leverages your **strengths**, and delivers your **message** in a way that is authentic and compelling.

Let's move beyond the myth of the universal solution and embrace the power of marketing individuality.

Case Study: The PPC Misstep and Tailored Turnaround

Pay-per-click (PPC) advertising stands as a beacon of promise, offering visibility, traffic, and the allure of rapid growth. And there's a valid reason why: it's easy to use and provides a ton of data that was previously not available about the effectiveness of paid campaigns. However, without a strategy that's closely aligned with a business's unique needs and customer journey, PPC can quickly become a costly misadventure.

What this client experienced illustrates this point vividly—a scenario where PPC advertising, though well-intentioned, was starkly misaligned with the business's actual needs, leading to numerous costly issues.

The Misaligned PPC Strategy

Sunset Self-Storage was looking to increase sales (aren't we all!). The initial strategy was straightforward: invest in PPC campaigns targeting broad, high-traffic keywords believed to be relevant to the largest possible audience in a specific geographic area.

So, they hired a self-proclaimed expert to set up their campaigns, and implementation was swift, with ads crafted and launched, bidding on popular terms within the geographic market and industry. That part they definitely got right.

Sunset had been running Google PPC ads for a couple of years by the time they came to me to assist with overall marketing strategy and had been spending around $4,500 per month; in total over $100K for these ads by the time they called me. Not a small sum for a small business.

The Resulting Issues

The issues surfaced almost as quickly as the ads went live ... *but no one noticed*. The person they outsourced to never bothered to check, or perhaps didn't know how or what to check. Neither did the entrepreneur.

The broad targeting did lead to a surge in clicks to their website, and this increased traffic was the only thing they really noticed; yet the conversion rate was abysmally low. The ads were reaching a wide audience, *but not the right audience*.

Of course, these wrong clicks cost them each time someone visited the link, so the ad cost soared and the return on investment (ROI[4]) plummeted. Sunset Self-Storage found itself paying for clicks that rarely converted into sales, draining resources.

---

4 ROI: The ultimate report card for your spending. It answers the age-old question: "Did I make more money than I spent, or is it time to go back to the drawing board?"

Corrective Actions and Lessons Learned

One of the concerns the client brought to me was the result from her personal searching on Google for the Sprouts store in her town and noticed that her company's ad came up as a result of that search. That's when she called me. It's important to note that her business is NOTHING remotely related to Sprouts, to food, to grocery at all, and her ads should not be shown when someone is searching for Sprouts. Recognizing the disconnect, I went in for a deeper look.

It immediately became clear that the broad keywords were too generic. Over half of the search phrases that had resulted in their ad being shown were not remotely related to the business. People don't always pay close attention and just click on the first result, which was her ad.

Half of their $4,500 monthly ad budget was spent on clicks from someone who was not remotely interested in their product or service.

Not only was their ad being found when searching for Sprouts and other retail stores … they were getting a majority of clicks from other countries such as Russia and China (people who could never even use the business unless they were moving to the area), plus other terms were also getting traction and costing money—terms which her business did NOT want their company to be associated with—including:

- demon for sale in (town) - hopefully they meant the Dodge vehicle, right? And not like … a devil demon?

- sex machines for rent - this means already used?!? I hope they sanitize!

- shop that sells sex pills in (town)

But my very favorite had to be this gem:

"Dr R_____ M_____ in (town) Google just give me the goddamn number"

I feel you, dude.

The first change we made: target the right geographic area by *excluding* other countries, not simply only targeting their city.

Next we added a ton of unwanted phrases to their negative keyword list. Phrases for which we don't want people shown the ad when they're searching for these terms. All those phrases that had been used, clicked upon, and cost the company money in the past year…Sprouts. Demons. Goddamn numbers.

This shift not only reduced the cost per click due to less competition, but also improved the quality of the traffic. Over $27,000 of their annual ad budget was spent on these incorrect clicks, and by taking care of the bad keyword problem, *we immediately saved them that much per year*. (There were additional things we did that saved even more.)

This was found money that they could use to target more the right people—people more likely to convert—or even for other needs in their business, including money in the owner's pocket!

The lessons this entrepreneur learned were invaluable:

- First ... always use a professional. If you initially use someone with less experience, that's not always bad, but you may want someone with more to give it a review.
- Broad reach does not necessarily equate to high-quality leads. Quality > Quantity
- Understanding the customer's *search intent* is crucial in PPC ads.
- Tailored, specific keyword targeting, and at the same time regularly updating negative keyword lists, can lead to better alignment with business goals.

Marketing Mirror

Think of a time when a popular marketing strategy did not work for your business. What could have been the reason?

How does your business culture and ethos influence your marketing strategies?

List some of the core values of your business:

List some of the unique qualities of your business:

> For each value or quality, what is one way that you could translate that into a specific marketing message or strategy?

The Funnel Fallacy

The concept of the sales funnel is often revered as the choreography to marketing success—a series of steps leading the customer gracefully from awareness to purchase. (Excuse me while I make some barely veiled reference to my love of dancing!)

However, there's a pervasive misconception that there's a one-size-fits-all funnel, a universal solution that every business can adopt for guaranteed results.

I hear this most often when an entrepreneur says, "**I need a funnel**". Someone has told them they need a funnel. You may have had someone tell you this as well.

I remind the entrepreneur that, if they are making ANY sales, *they already have a funnel*. **What someone is selling them on is a *funnel software platform*.**

This belief - *that you must use specific software* - is the funnel fallacy, and it's time to address why it's a flawed approach.

The Misconception of the Universal Funnel

The traditional marketing funnel model suggests a linear journey: awareness, interest, decision, and action.

While this model provides a foundational understanding of consumer behavior, the fallacy lies in the assumption that every business can apply the same funnel structure with equal effectiveness, and that it requires specific software to do so.

"Sales funnels" have been around since the dawn of time, and until relatively recently in the big scheme of history, no software or technology was ever used. When I was starting my first full-time job in advertising, I was using index cards and a "tickler" system. Once software became more prevalent, and long before others were using it, I found ways for tech to complement other methods. I was ridiculously successful at advertising sales, and later at nonprofit fundraising. Not once did I need to use a "sales funnel" software platform; heck, they barely existed early in my career.

Throw in the software that the latest person is touting, and you hear that you need upsells and downsells and gates and lead magnets and video sales pages and, and, and … Nope. Not necessarily.

The reality is that no two businesses are alike, and the funnel that works for one may be entirely unsuitable for another.

The Essential Nature of Bespoke Funnels

Software funnels are indeed helpful; they can provide a framework for nurturing leads and guiding potential customers towards making a purchase.

However, the design of these funnels must be as unique as the business model and the audience it serves. A B2B[5] enterprise with a long sales cycle requires a vastly different

---

5 B2B (Business to Business): Here, your audience is other businesses, usually with a fairly long sales cycle. It's a conversation between corporate entities, often centered around long-term solutions and partnerships. This audience usually has several layers of approvals; the person you're speaking to who is interested in your product usually is not the final approval, it may need to go through management, accounting and others.

funnel approach compared to a B2C[6] e-commerce platform that thrives on impulse purchases. And B2P[7] (Business to Professional) falls somewhere in the middle.

What is clear is that understanding your customer's journey is paramount, and then you will have a better understanding of how your funnel needs to work. A funnel should not be a rigid construct, but a fluid and adaptable pathway that reflects the actual steps your unique customers take from discovering your brand to becoming loyal advocates. This might include technology, and also likely does not require any specific funnel platform.

The Bespoke Approach

To design a funnel that resonates with your audience, start by mapping out the customer journey specific to your business. Identify the touchpoints where customers engage with your brand from the very first point in time that they

---

6 B2C (Business to Consumer): This is where you're talking directly to the everyday person, the end-user. It's about understanding and appealing to individual needs, desires, and emotions, making each consumer feel like your product or service was made just for them. Usually a relatively short sales cycle, sometimes with immediate purchases.

7 You won't hear this term as much, because some marketers aren't even aware of the nuances of different types of audiences and their unique sales cycles. B2P (Business to Professional): When you're selling not just to businesses or consumers, but to the savvy entrepreneur. It's like having a conversation with someone who speaks your own secret business language. The sales process is usually somewhere between B2C and B2C.

become aware of your business, the questions they have at each stage, and the barriers they might face to purchasing.

- ☐ Is there anything missing?
- ☐ Anything awkward?
- ☐ Anything redundant?
- ☐ Anywhere that things tend to fall through the cracks unless we have some automated follow up?

Use this information to create a funnel that addresses these specific elements, ensuring that each stage is optimized to move the customer closer to a sale.

The funnel fallacy can lead businesses to adopt marketing strategies (and sometimes buy expensive software) that are misaligned with their needs and, more importantly, the needs of their customers. By understanding the importance of a tailored funnel, businesses can create a more effective and efficient pathway to conversion, one that respects the unique aspects of their brand and the people they serve.

Case Study: The Funnel That Just Didn't Fit

Most of the well-known "funnel systems" that you've probably been told that you MUST use specialize in *B2C products*.

I was working with a B2P (Business-to-Professional) service company that we will call TeamSync Solutions, a consulting firm specializing in corporate in-house professional development, which found itself grappling with an underperforming marketing funnel that they were having trouble integrating with the existing software they had been using for years.

The firm had initially adopted a funnel strategy modeled after a well-known MLM-type marketing system, renowned for its success in direct sales and rapid conversion tactics. This system, while effective in certain industries, was not yielding the expected results for the nuanced field of their professional services.

Identifying the Misfit

The signs that the existing funnel was not a good fit were clear:

- **Low Conversion Rates:** Despite high traffic, the conversion rates were abysmally low. The quick-sale tactics of the funnel did not resonate with the professional clientele who required trust-building and a more consultative sales approach. Whenever I get the question from an entrepreneur about what to do when they have good traffic and poor sales, I tell them to look at what's on the page; the visitor isn't getting what they expected to see, somehow.
- **High Drop-off before the Consultation Stage:** The funnel led to a free consultation offer to get the visitor connected with their sales team, but the drop-off rate post-consultation was high. The system failed to nurture leads effectively through the decision-making process typical of professional services. The offer was too soon.

- **Incongruent Messaging:** The language and style of the funnel were more aggressive and sales-oriented, which clashed with the firm's brand of personalized and client-focused service.
- **Doubling of Effort and Expense:** I'm a firm believer that technology should always *work for you*, and in this case, the new funnel that the consultant had set up was causing double the work. The team was having to manually take data from the funnel system and plug it into their internal CRM, email, bookkeeping and other systems ... and then manually do it in the opposite direction as well.

Developing a Suitable Funnel

We helped them tackle a strategic overhaul of their funnel to better align with their B2P model by taking these steps:

- **In-depth Audience Analysis:** We began with deep research into their target audience, understanding the unique decision-making processes of professionals and the factors that influenced their trust and commitment. We found that it was NOT the "$7 lead magnet" with upsells that the previous consultant had set up and not a single prospect ever purchased.
- **Content-Driven Strategy:** Recognizing the need for thought leadership in their field, the new funnel was designed to offer valuable content at each stage, establishing credibility and nurturing leads with industry insights, case studies, and testimonials.

- **Consultative Approach:** The revised funnel introduced multiple touchpoints for personalized interactions, replacing a single offer and its awkward "upsells" with a series of webinars, Q&A sessions, and, most importantly, bespoke personal follow-ups by their existing sales team.
- **Long-Term Relationship Building:** The focus shifted from immediate product-like sales to long-term relationship building, with email sequences that provided ongoing value and engagement beyond the initial contact.

Implementation and Results

The implementation of the new funnel form TeamSync involved a comprehensive content creation plan using strategies that they already had in place, connecting with their existing CRM system to manage the complex lead nurturing sequences, and training for the sales team on the new consultative approach.

An extra piece we added was a repository of similar email content that the sales team could easily grab and forward to a prospect they were speaking to, helping provide the right message at the right time individually.

The results were transformative:

- **Increased Conversion Rates:** The conversion rates from lead to client saw a significant increase, as the new funnel resonated with the professional audience's desire for expertise and trust.

- **Higher Engagement:** The engagement levels throughout the funnel improved, with more professionals attending interacting with the distinct types of content provided.
- **Brand Alignment:** The messaging and tactics now aligned with the firm's brand values, enhancing their reputation in the industry.
- **Saving Money and Time:** The new process was more streamlined and removed all of the manual duplication that they were needing to do, plus allowed them to cancel unnecessary subscriptions for technology that duplicated other platforms they were already using.

Oh, and that $7 "product" they had created? They started giving it away free as part of the process.

This case study illustrates the importance of aligning any marketing funnel with the business model and the audience it serves. By moving away from a one-size-fits-all funnel and developing a strategy tailored to the B2P service industry, the consultancy firm was able to engage more effectively with their professional clientele and achieve substantial growth.

Recognizing Your Unique Marketing Needs

Recognizing and adapting to your unique marketing needs is not just a strategy—it's a survival skill. As your business evolves, so too should your marketing strategies.

The key is to remain vigilant and responsive to the **signs that your current approach may need a refresh** or a complete overhaul.

Here's a guide to help you assess your marketing needs and a checklist to determine if your current strategy still aligns with your business goals.

Assessment Guide

- **Reflect on Your Business Goals:** Have your business objectives shifted since you last devised your marketing strategy? Ensure your marketing efforts are in lockstep with your current goals.
- **Analyze Your Target Audience:** Has your target audience's behavior changed? Are there new customer segments you haven't considered before? Understanding your audience is critical to effective marketing.
- **Evaluate Your Brand Positioning:** Consider whether your brand's message is still resonating with your audience. Is your unique value proposition clear and compelling in your marketing materials?
- **Review Your Metrics:** Look at your key performance indicators (KPIs[8]). Are you meeting your targets? If not, it might be time to pivot your strategy.

---

8 KPIs are the scoreboard of the business world. These figures tell you if you're winning the game or if it's time to call a timeout and rethink your strategy.

- **Consider Market Trends:** Are there new trends or technologies that could impact your marketing effectiveness? Stay current and be ready to adapt to maintain a competitive edge.

Evaluate if Your Strategy is as Unique as Your Business

Alignment with Business Goals:

- Does your marketing strategy support your current business objectives?
- Are your marketing efforts contributing to your bottom line?

Audience Engagement:

- Are you reaching your target audience effectively?
- Is your audience engaging with your content?
- Have you noticed a decline in engagement or conversion rates?

Brand Messaging:

- Does your marketing communicate your brand's unique value proposition clearly?
- Is your brand voice consistent across all marketing channels?

Competitive Position:

- How does your marketing strategy stack up against your competitors?
- Are you leveraging your competitive advantages in your marketing?

Marketing ROI:

- Are you getting a good return on investment for your marketing spend?
- Which marketing channels are yielding the best results?

Adaptability and Innovation:

- Is your marketing strategy flexible enough to adapt to market changes?
- Are you incorporating new marketing trends and technologies that could benefit your business?

Customer Feedback:

- What is the feedback from your customers regarding your marketing? Is it positive, or are there areas for improvement?
- Do you have a system to regularly collect and review feedback?

Sales Funnel Efficiency:

- Is your sales funnel optimized for conversion at each stage?
- Are there any stages in the funnel where prospects drop off more than they should?

Operational:

- Is there anywhere that you are currently having to double the work?
- Are there any redundant software or tools you're paying for or using (or paying for and not using)?
- Are you making a profit (not just revenue), and is at a level that it can sustain your business?

If you find that your current marketing strategy is not ticking the right boxes, it may be time to pivot and tailor a novel approach that better suits your evolving business needs.

Remember, the most effective marketing strategies are bespoke strategies that are as unique as the businesses they serve. Don't hesitate to reach out for professional guidance to navigate this process and ensure that your marketing efforts are as effective and efficient as possible.

Transitioning to a Bespoke Approach

Shifting from a generic to a customized marketing strategy is akin to tailoring a suit—it must fit perfectly to look its best. A bespoke marketing strategy not only fits your business's current needs but also adapts to future growth and changes in the market.

Here's how you can transition to a strategy that's cut just for you.

Steps to Customize Your Marketing Strategy

- **Deep Research Data:** Use your business data to inform your decisions. Look at customer behaviors, purchase patterns, and feedback to understand what works and what doesn't.

- **Engage with Your Audience:** Have conversations with your customers. Use surveys, social media interactions, and direct feedback to gain insights into their needs and preferences.

- **Analyze Competitors:** Understand your competitors' strategies and identify gaps that your business can fill. This can help you find your unique angle in the market.

- **Set Clear Objectives:** Define what success looks like for your business. Set SMART (Specific, Measurable, Achievable, Relevant, Time-bound) goals that are bespoke to your business's vision.

- **Test and Learn:** Implement small-scale tests to see what resonates with your audience. Use A/B testing for campaigns to refine messaging, offers, and channels.

- **Iterate Quickly:** Be prepared to make quick changes based on what the data tells you (but without completely stopping any strategy - they still need time to vet). Flexibility is key in adapting to what's effective.

- **Seek Professional Insight:** Sometimes, an external perspective can provide clarity. Consider consulting with a marketing expert to help tailor your strategy. This doesn't always require a long-term commitment; for example, I offer individual Fractional CMO[9] sessions for this purpose.

Importance of Flexibility and Adaptation

- **Stay Relevant:** Markets and consumer behaviors are constantly changing. A flexible marketing plan can quickly adapt to these changes, keeping your business relevant.
- **Innovate Continuously:** Flexibility encourages innovation. It allows you to experiment with innovative ideas and technologies that can give you a competitive edge.
- **Manage Resources Efficiently:** Adaptation helps you allocate resources to the most effective strategies, ensuring a better return on investment.

Embracing Marketing Diversity

Throughout our journey so far, we've uncovered the perils of the one-size-fits-all marketing myth. The key takeaways are clear: what works for one business may not work for

---

9 Imagine having a marketing superhero on speed dial, ready to swoop in with a cape of experience and a toolkit of strategies, but only when you need them. That's a Fractional Chief Marketing Officer for you! It's like renting a slice of a top-tier marketing brain, giving you access to years of wisdom, insights, and expertise, without the full-time executive price tag. Need a marketing mastermind for just an hour or two? No problem - a Fractional CMO is your go-to expert for big-picture thinking in bite-sized appointments. Perfect for when you want the brains without full-time commitment.

another, and the diversity of your business should be mirrored in your marketing efforts.

Embrace Your Business Uniqueness

- **Celebrate Your Individuality:** Your business has a unique story, value proposition, and audience. Your marketing should celebrate and communicate this individuality.
- **Customize Your Tactics:** Use the insights you've gained about your business to develop marketing tactics that speak directly to your audience's needs and desires.
- **Innovate with Confidence:** Don't be afraid to try new approaches. Innovation is not just for the big players; it's accessible to all businesses willing to adapt and experiment.

Encouragement for the Reader

Throughout this book and your entrepreneurial journey, keep in mind that the most successful marketing strategies are those that mirror the distinctiveness and dynamism of the businesses they serve. Embrace the diversity of your business, and let your marketing reflect that richness and variety.

I encourage you to step away from the generic and step into a world where your marketing is a perfect fit for your business.

Key Takeaways

- Reject the myth of universal solutions. Focus on creating marketing strategies that are customized to your unique business needs.

- Understand why the allure of one-size-fits-all strategies is misleading and recognize the importance of bespoke solutions for your business.

- Acknowledge and leverage the unique aspects of your business in your marketing approach, steering clear of generic strategies.

- Learn the art of customizing marketing strategies to suit your specific business goals, audience, and industry nuances.

The DIY Dilemma

Ahhh … the frontier of entrepreneurial autonomy, where the allure of DIY marketing beckons with promises of cost savings, control, and that invaluable personal touch.

In this section, we're not painting by numbers; we're exploring the full spectrum of marketing's hues and shades, understanding that while the DIY approach may seem like a canvas of opportunity, it often **requires a more skilled hand** to create a masterpiece. (And herein lies my nod to my passion for art).

We'll delve into the initial appeal of DIY marketing for entrepreneurs. You'll discover why rolling up your sleeves and taking charge of your marketing can seem like the golden ticket to branding success. We'll discuss the **common misconception** that marketing, with all its intricacies, is as simple as following a recipe—a pinch of SEO here, a dash of social media there, and voilà, success! (If only it were that easy!)

But as we'll soon uncover, the reality of DIY marketing is fraught with challenges that are not immediately apparent. We'll highlight the **risks of oversimplification** and the potential for costly mistakes that can arise from a lack of specialized knowledge. From the nuances of constant algorithm changes to the subtleties of brand voice, the complexities of marketing are as varied as they are vast.

We'll examine a case study of a business that faced setbacks due to DIY website development. The tale will unfold, revealing SEO mishaps, user experience faux pas, and the tangible (and shocking) impact on the business's bottom line. It's a cautionary tale that underscores the importance of expertise in the digital age.

A common trap many entrepreneurs fall into is to continue DIY marketing even when it becomes a roadblock to growth.

While I often work with solo startup entrepreneurs, I also work with those who have already passed that initial stage and are hell-bent on creating their first million-dollar-revenue year. What they all learn on the journey to 7-figures, without fail, is that to reach that level, *you can't do the same things you did to reach the level before* - and this includes DIYing your marketing.

The better strategy is recognizing when it's time to seek professional help to elevate your marketing efforts from a solo struggle to a collaborative success. **Recognizing when it's time** to call in the professionals is crucial, and we'll provide guidance on identifying those signs. We'll discuss the invaluable contributions that professional marketers bring to the table—insights that go beyond simply avoiding errors.

And for those ready to make the shift from DIY to guided expertise, we'll offer advice on how to transition smoothly, ensuring that the marketing professional you choose is not just a service provider but a partner who respects and understands your vision.

As we conclude this section, we'll summarize the key insights on the challenges and limitations of DIY marketing. We'll reinforce the message that seeking professional help is not a sign of failure but a step towards maturity and success in your marketing journey.

And so, I invite you to take a moment to evaluate your current marketing efforts if you haven't already done so in the prior section. Consider the benefits of professional guidance, and if you find yourself at a crossroads, reach out for a marketing consultation. Together, you and your expert can navigate the complexities of marketing and chart a course that aligns with the unique vision and values of your business.

Let's embark on this path to marketing maturity, leaving behind the DIY dilemma, and embracing the expertise that can elevate your brand to new heights.

The Allure of DIY Marketing

There's a certain charm to the do-it-yourself approach. You're drawn to the promise of cost savings, the allure of complete control, and the personal touch that only you can infuse into your brand. It's the entrepreneurial dream: steering your ship single-handedly through the waters of commerce, your hand on the marketing wheel, charting your own course to success. This is the initial siren call of DIY marketing, beckoning with the sweet whispers of independence and the pride of self-sufficiency.

The common misconception, however, is that marketing is a straightforward task, one that can be executed with ease by anyone willing to put in the time. It's an attractive notion, especially in a world where a vast sea of information is at our fingertips and every tool we could imagine is readily available.

Many entrepreneurs believe that with a bit of quick research and some intuitive tools, they can master the art of marketing and *skip the need to invest in specialized knowledge.*

After all, who knows your unique business better than you?

The Reality of DIY Marketing Challenges

Yet, beneath this appealing veneer lies a complex web of intricacies that form the backbone of effective marketing. The reality is that **marketing is a multifaceted discipline**, blending creativity with analytics, intuition with data, and strategy with spontaneity. It's not just about creating eye-catching ads or posting regularly on social media; it's about understanding consumer behavior, market trends, SEO, content strategy, brand positioning, and so much more.

The **risks of oversimplification** are many. Entrepreneurs can find themselves pouring time and resources into strategies that yield little return, not because of a lack of effort, but because of a lack of expertise or from having chosen the wrong strategy. The digital landscape is particularly unforgiving, with its ever-changing algorithms and the constant evolution of best practices. What worked yesterday may not work today, and keeping abreast of these changes requires a dedication that can become overwhelming for those trying to juggle all of the other aspects of their business.

Just for SEO alone, our team members spend multiple hours every week keeping up with the latest changes, and this is becoming even more true with the recent looming switch to AI search. For most entrepreneurs, this is not where their Zone of Genius[10] does, or should, reside.

The potential for costly mistakes is significant. Missteps in branding can lead to a disjointed business identity, while errors in targeting can result in advertising dollars evaporating into the ether - as already mentioned. Poorly managed SEO can bury your website under pages of search results, and a lack of conversion strategy can turn a stream of traffic into a trickle of lost opportunities.

---

10 Zone of Genius: That sweet spot where your skills and passions collide, creating an explosion of productivity and satisfaction. It's the business equivalent of hitting every green light on your way to work. The portion of your business that only you can do.

Marketing Mirror

Assess your current marketing skills and resources. What are the areas you excel in, and where could you use professional help?

_____

_____

Is marketing your personal Zone of Genius?

_____

What are your biggest obstacles in achieving effective marketing? Is it knowledge, time, resources, or something else?

_____

_____

Self-Assessment

Answer Yes or No to each question. Remember, there are no right or wrong answers, this is simply a self-assessment.

	YES	NO
Do you have a clear and we–defined brand voice and message that others can understand?	☐	☐
Have you been disappointed by the results of past marketing efforts, either done by you or by a vendor?	☐	☐
Are you using a "Virtual Assistant" for your marketing, but find yourself spending more time managing the process than you would like?	☐	☐
Do you have specific, expert marketing skills within your business?	☐	☐
Do you have sufficient time to dedicate to learning, developing and executing a marketing strategy?	☐	☐

Do you have access to all of the marketing resources (tools, software, etc.) needed to effectively market your business?   ☐   ☐

Are you able to keep up with the latest marketing trends and technologies, along with your day-to-day work?   ☐   ☐

Do you feel confident in your ability to measure and analyze the ROI of your marketing efforts?   ☐   ☐

Are you confident that you're using the most effective marketing strategies for your business?   ☐   ☐

Scoring:

Mostly 'Yes': You may have the necessary resources and skills to handle marketing internally. However, consider outsourcing specific aspects where you answered 'No'.

Mostly 'No': It's likely in your best interest to outsource your marketing. Look for professional help, especially in areas where you lack expertise, time, or resources.

Personal Anecdote: A Journey Through DIY Marketing

Embarking on the DIY marketing path can often feel like setting sail on a solo voyage — the thrill of the open sea, the autonomy in navigation, and the pride of personal endeavor. But as I've learned through my own experiences, even a seasoned marketer can encounter rough waters when trying to handle every aspect of marketing single-handedly.

As I was starting my own business as a solo entrepreneur (at least this round; this isn't the first time I've been a CEO), I took on the task of managing my own social media along with everything else. It seemed logical; who could possibly convey my vision and voice better than myself? Plus, in addition to being a marketing expert, since I was a solo entrepreneur at that time, I was also the only person around to do it. Sure, I could have outsourced to a freelancer, but the ones I was finding had *vastly less experience than I did*; and when I tried once or twice realized that I was having to spend too much time teaching them how to do the job.

It was a journey that began with enthusiasm, armed with the latest tools and strategies, ready to engage with my audience directly.

However, as my business grew, so did the demands on my time. Social media, with its relentless need for fresh content, regular engagement, and constant monitoring, began to encroach upon the hours I had reserved for my zone of genius—those activities where my expertise could shine and bring the most value to my clients. **I found myself in a paradox**: a marketing expert caught in the web of executing marketing tasks, leaving less time for the strategic thinking and creative work that only I could do.

It was a pivotal moment, one that led to a significant realization with perfect timing since I had some strong team members now in place. **Even though I had the expertise** to manage my own social media didn't mean I should. The decision to let my team take over was not an easy one; it felt akin to handing over a set of keys to my own kingdom. But in doing so, I discovered the power of delegation and focus. By entrusting this aspect of my marketing to capable hands, I was able to reclaim time which I could then focus elsewhere.

This shift didn't just free up my schedule; **it transformed my approach to my own business**. It also took some weight off my shoulders. I was able to dive deeper into the work that fueled my passion and drove my business forward. My team, armed with their own expertise, brought new life and perspectives to our social media presence, often exceeding my own expectations.

The lesson here was clear: DIY marketing, while initially cost-effective and personal, can become a hindrance to growth if it pulls you away from your core strengths; away from your Zone of Genius. It's about recognizing when to hold on and when to let go, understanding that sometimes *the best way to amplify your voice is to let others help you project it*.

And it's also about choosing the most effective piece to outsource first—which entrepreneurs often get wrong (and I'll speak about that more later).

For entrepreneurs navigating the DIY marketing seas, remember that your time is precious, and your 'zone of genius' is where you can make the most significant waves in your business that no one else can. Don't shy away from seeking help, be it from your team or external experts. It's not just about managing tasks; **it's about steering your business towards its greatest potential.**

Case Study: The Website Woes

A company's website is often its first impression, its storefront, and its salesperson all rolled into one. The tale of one particular business serves as a cautionary case study on the perils of entrusting this critical asset to inexperienced hands.

This business, which we will call "Timeless Treasures" is driven by a vision to carve out a unique space in the market, decided to take the mostly DIY route for website redevelopment—moving from a strictly html-base site (it was old!) to one on WordPress with WooCommerce, an industry standard that allows for great expansion in functionality.

In their case, it wasn't fully DIY; they hired an acquaintance even though that person had only ever built one website— their own for a hobby. But from that standpoint it was very similar to DIY. The initial appeal was understandable: cost savings (although not a lot; they still paid a noticeable pricetag), control, and the belief that an excited first-time builder could translate into a compelling online presence. However, the complexities of web development and SEO soon turned this digital dream into a costly nightmare, despite WordPress being one of the easiest platforms to work with.

The issues began with fundamental major SEO mishaps. The website, though aesthetically pleasing enough, was built without a solid understanding of the technology underlying any site. They were moving their ecommerce business from one platform to a better one, primarily because the old one was NOT mobile responsive, which should have provided a better experience and increased their traffic and sales.

There were a couple of serious issues that destroyed their website. We're not talking about trivial things like meta tags, alt attributes, and keyword optimization. When I look at SEO, those aren't the things I consider first.

There was one point that they were attempting to get Google to see the updated version of a page (with a slightly different URL structure), and it was still finding the old version. This is pretty common since Google was taking 2-3 months to crawl new content at the time. In Googling the issue, the freelancer found some advice to put that URL into Google Search Console's "removal tool" in an attempt to force Google to find the new URL.

Unfortunately, they didn't understand the proper use of "wildcards" in the URL and added a * ... which tells Google to include everything after the asterisk. So while they should have used https://website.com/ to only remove the home page, they entered https://website.com/* *and thereby removed the entire website from Google's memory.*

When the business came to me to fix issues with their website, not understanding why it wasn't appearing on Google any more *at all* (and the freelancer no longer responding to months of calls and emails, perhaps realizing how out of their depth they were) ... I found the removal issue as soon as they added access for me to their Google Search Console.

The client had been running this ecommerce store website for close to 20 years and tons of historical SEO "juice" built up over that time. They went from making six figures a year in their ecommerce business to their website not appearing at all and **zero income almost overnight**.

I deleted those removal requests, but by then the damage had already been done. No recovering from this ... it was a case of having to start all SEO efforts over again from scratch, and competing against other businesses that had never removed their websites from Google and therefore now had a stronger presence with more history.

User experience suffered as well. The site's navigation was confusing, the load times were terrible (5 minutes to load a page!! Even I didn't want to wait that long, and I was paid to!), and, while one of the major reasons they switched was to get a mobile responsive site, the mobile experience was not fully considered, all leading to a high bounce rate.

The on-site search was also trashed. I don't know of a better way to put that. WordPress and WooCommerce both have robust built-in search algorithms, but for some reason custom code was added that just tanked those on-site search capabilities.

Customers who did find the site were often quick to leave, frustrated by the inability to find what they were looking for with ease.

The impact on the business was immediate and severe. The website, which was supposed to be an engine for growth, became a barrier to it.

It took months of meticulous work to undo the damage. (Yes, the repairs could have been much quicker, but the entrepreneur now had a limited monthly budget … so projects were finished as their budget allowed). Overhauling the site's structure, ensuring that it was intuitive, responsive, and accessible. SEO best practices were implemented, from on-page optimizations to a content strategy designed to attract and engage the target audience. Specific tech fixes to improve site speed (from an F to an A+ on Google site speed).

As the website began to climb the search rankings again, traffic and sales followed. The improved user experience led to longer visits, more engagement, and, crucially, conversions. The business was not just back to making money; it was on a path to growth that had previously been blocked by a well-intentioned but misguided DIY approach.

This case study underscores the importance of professional expertise, especially *when tech is involved*. It's a stark reminder that while the DIY route may seem appealing, the potential for costly mistakes and setbacks is high. For businesses looking to make their mark online, investing in professional services is not just a wise choice; it's an essential one.

Common DIY Marketing Mistakes

While web presence and social media are critical components of modern marketing, the essence of marketing mistakes often lies in the very basics of business strategy.

Here are some foundational missteps that I see entrepreneurs who DIY their marketing frequently encounter, including product misalignment, audience misidentification, and misconceptions about niche marketing.

Letting Someone Else Hold the Keys to the Kingdom

One critical mistake many entrepreneurs frequently make simply because they have never been told not to, is relinquishing too much control over their digital assets. This often happens in the context of website management and domain ownership. This often happens when you're paying a freelance web designer (or whichever related title they use) a monthly fee that includes your setup, design, hosting and more.

It's akin to building your castle on someone else's land.

Domain name (URL). Your domain name is your digital address, the cornerstone of your online identity. It's surprising how many business owners allow their web developer or a third party to register their domain name. This is risky for several reasons. If the person who registered your domain disappears or becomes uncooperative, you could lose access to your website and email. It's like handing the keys to your storefront to someone else and hoping they'll always let you in.

Hosting control. Another common issue arises when businesses let their web person own or control their website hosting. This scenario can lead to numerous problems, especially if you decide to part ways with that service provider. You might find yourself unable to access your website, update content, or even make essential security updates. It's as if you're renting your business space and suddenly find the doors locked with your goods inside.

Stealing SEO. A particularly insidious tactic is when a web developer, or SEO expert (I've seen this one done by both) sets up a secondary website for "SEO purposes." Sometimes the business owner doesn't even realize this was done, and just assumes the work is on their existing website. What the expert does is optimize this other website (which then *competes against* your existing website!) and pays for ads to send leads to that second site. Then they have you pay per lead which they provide you (plus sometimes a flat monthly fee).

It's like opening a second store right next door with the same name but inferior products—it just doesn't make sense to you or your customers.

But it does make sense to the freelancer.

When you later realize that you were actually paying for leads going to a different website (that you don't own and probably don't have access to), and decide to fire the freelancer, they turn around and *sell that site to your competitor*. And all of that 'SEO' you've been paying for months or years, is now directly benefiting some other company. Keep in mind, usually when you pay for SEO work, it benefits your website long-term. It's one of the strategies that keeps giving. But not when it's being done on a site that you don't own.

The person this strategy is benefiting is the freelancer. And whenever there is a marketing strategy that benefits the freelancer more than it benefits you should be a red flag.

Misunderstanding the Product's Market Fit:

One of the cardinal sins of marketing is not fully understanding how your product fits into the market. An example of this is launching a product based on personal passion without validating market demand, leading to misaligned expectations and potential failure.

To create a business that generates a profit—which is the ONLY thing that can provide you with a living and keep the doors open—you need three things:

1. To sell a product or service that people want,

2. which is something they will actually buy/pay for,

3. and that they will individually pay enough, or there will be enough overall purchases, to sustain your business.

Too many budding entrepreneurs miss one or more of those, and doing so is a recipe for failure.

Misidentifying the Target Audience:

Knowing your audience is Marketing 101, yet many entrepreneurs make assumptions without research and tend to focus on their product or service first. That is, after all, how so many businesses are started—an entrepreneur with an idea for a product or service.

Not having a solid understanding of the audience (and making sure it's the RIGHT audience) can result in messaging that doesn't resonate, wasted ad spend, and a product that doesn't quite meet the needs of any specific group.

Misconceptions About Your Niche:

The advice to "niche down" can be sound (when done right) but **misunderstanding what that "having a niche" means** can be detrimental. Niching should be about focusing on an area where you can excel and serve a specific audience, not restricting your business so much that growth becomes impossible.

What you hear often, but what is NOT a niche, is something like "I serve _____ by _____". Something like "I serve female creatives by helping them develop bookkeeping processes." The proper term for this particular descriptive would be *target audience* paired with your services. Your business will likely have a couple of target audiences. A target audience is not a niche; although it can become the target audience because of a niche. It's really not as effective the other way around.

"Find your niche" is one of those cookie-cutter strategies that don't work for everyone, or for anyone when done wrong for that matter.

So, what is a niche? A niche is actually *a small corner of a market where you are likely the only provider (or one of less than a handful).* This can also equate to having a small audience, but not always.

Overcomplicating the Marketing Message:

Simplicity is key in communication. Entrepreneurs have often complicated their messaging, trying to include too much information—everything plus the kitchen sink, or using jargon that confuses the audience.

Ignoring the Competition:

While you shouldn't obsess over competitors, ignoring them is a mistake. DIY marketers often fail to conduct a competitive analysis, which can provide insights into what works and what gaps you can fill.

Failing to Test and Iterate:

Marketing is an iterative process. Many entrepreneurs stick to a "set it and forget it" mentality, not realizing that testing and adapting is crucial for finding what resonates with the audience. White I always recommend that you let a strategy run long enough to collect solid data (and I will speak about that more later), you also can't let it go forever without a strategic revisit.

Lack of a Unique Service Proposition:

Without a clear USP[11] it's hard to stand out in a crowded market. DIY marketers sometimes struggle to articulate

---

11 Your USP is like your business's secret sauce, that special ingredient that makes your customers choose you over anyone else. It's the superhero cape your brand wears, making it stand out in a sea of sameness. Whether it's your unmatched customer service, an innovative product feature, or a unique pricing structure, your USP is what makes your business not just a choice, but the choice. It's your business's fingerprint, unique and identifying, leaving a memorable impression on your customers.

what makes their offering unique, leading to a lack of differentiation. Too many have so many USPs they focus on that each one becomes watered down.

A related mistake is trying to make price your differentiator. Those businesses that try to be the lowest cost leader are usually also the first to close (unless they're so huge that they can eat a lot of low profit points).

Inconsistent Customer Experience:

The customer journey should be seamless across all touchpoints. DIY efforts often result in a disjointed experience, eroding trust and brand loyalty.

Nothing is worse than being a consumer who chats with support online to get an answer, and then later when they call get a completely different answer. Communications should be aligned across touchpoints.

Underestimating the Importance of Brand Story:

A compelling brand story can be a powerful tool to connect with customers. DIY marketers often neglect this aspect, missing the opportunity to build a deeper relationship with their audience. Or get it wrong and focus on pieces of their personal story (which the audience doesn't always care about) versus the customer's story; or maintain their focus on design and graphic elements, which isn't always the most important aspect of your brand where focus should be directed.

Not Leveraging Customer Insights:

Your own customers are a wealth of information. Entrepreneurs who DIY their marketing sometimes fail to gather or act on customer insights, which can guide product development and marketing strategies.

Disregarding the Marketing Funnel:

Understanding the customer's journey from awareness to purchase is crucial. DIY marketers often focus only on the top or bottom of the funnel, leading to missed opportunities for nurturing leads.

Or, like we already discussed, focus on the software platform, when that alone isn't actually the funnel.

Overlooking Post-Purchase Engagement:

The relationship with a customer doesn't end at purchase. A common mistake entrepreneurs make is neglecting post-purchase engagement, which is essential for retention and word-of-mouth referrals (which is still the best marketing strategy around).

Inadequate Follow-Up:

Follow-up is key in converting leads to customers. Many DIY marketers fail to implement effective follow-up strategies, leading to a leaky sales pipeline.

Poor Pricing Strategies:

Pricing is a complex task that requires understanding value perception and cost structures. Many entrepreneurs set prices based on gut feeling rather than strategic analysis, which can impact profitability; and remember, **profit > revenue.**

Not Aligning Marketing with Sales:

Marketing and sales should work hand in hand, but DIY efforts often result in a disconnect between the two, causing friction and lost opportunities. Sales is actually a function of marketing, and it should all work seamlessly together, even when it's technically handled by separate departments.

Ignoring Legal and Ethical Guidelines:

Marketing is not just about creativity; it's also about compliance. DIY marketers sometimes overlook legal requirements like copyright laws (no, you can't use an image just because you found it on Google), privacy regulations, and advertising standards, which can lead to serious repercussions.

Recognizing the Need for Professional Help

As an entrepreneur, you're accustomed to wearing many hats, but there comes a time when the marketing cap becomes too complex or time-consuming to wear effectively. Recognizing the need for professional marketing help is a pivotal moment in your business's growth. Here are signs that it's time to consider professional assistance:

- **Stagnant or Declining Growth:** If your growth plateaus or dips despite your marketing efforts, it's a clear indicator that your strategies may need a professional overhaul.
- **Overwhelm and Time Constraints:** When marketing tasks start to encroach on the time needed for core business activities, it's time to delegate to someone who can focus solely on marketing.
- **Inconsistent Brand Messaging:** If your brand voice and messaging are inconsistent across different channels, a professional can help streamline and maintain a cohesive brand identity.
- **Low Conversion Rates:** If your audience isn't converting at the expected rate, a marketing professional can pinpoint and address the issues in your sales funnel.
- **Difficulty in Scaling Up:** If you're ready to scale but unsure how to adjust your marketing accordingly, a professional can provide the strategic insight needed for growth.

- **Lack of Expertise in New Channels:** When expanding into new marketing channels or technologies, the learning curve can be steep. Professionals can navigate these with ease.
- **Marketing Feels Like a Burden:** If marketing feels more like a chore than an exciting part of your business, it's time to bring in someone who is passionate and skilled in this area.

The value that professional marketers bring extends far beyond avoiding mistakes. They provide strategic direction, ensure brand consistency, and use data-driven insights to optimize campaigns. They also bring creativity, fresh perspectives, and the ability to stay ahead of marketing trends, which can be invaluable to your business.

The One Question You Should Ask

A common question that entrepreneurs bring to me is "what should I post on social media?"

My answer is:

you're asking the wrong question.

If you always ask the wrong question, you will never get the right answer.

It's not about what you should post on social media, but if that's even the most effective spot to focus your marketing efforts.

And it's not what you should post on social media, but if YOU should even be the one posting in the first place.

Transitioning from DIY to Guided Expertise

When it comes to elevating your marketing efforts, the sequence in which you seek help can be just as crucial as the help itself.

One of the most common missteps that I see entrepreneurs make is making their first outsource hire a marketing Virtual Assistant (VA), thinking to offload some of the more routine marketing tasks they have been personally handling.

While anything to free up some of your precious time seems logical, in this case it's often putting the cart before the horse. A VA can indeed take repetitive tasks off your plate, but without a solid marketing strategy and a well-defined brand voice already in place, even the most efficient VA may not be able to contribute effectively to your business's growth.

A related issue I frequently see is an entrepreneur who has their brand voice and communication preferences *in their head*, but it's never been written and/or they don't yet have it focused where they can relay it to someone else *in a way that the person understands and can create in the same style*.

It's akin to hiring a crew to sail a ship without a course plotted; they can keep the vessel afloat, but without direction, you won't reach your desired destination. You might get somewhere, but it may not be where you actually wanted to go. And if you're constantly having to redirect them each few knots, you won't get very far very fast.

If a client doesn't have a solid brand voice and communication guide, I *always* recommend that we work on this first.

Transitioning to a bespoke marketing approach should begin with strategic guidance—a compass to navigate the vast marketing seas. Once you have a clear direction, then a VA can be a valuable asset in maintaining your course and speed.

Making the shift from DIY to professional marketing doesn't have to be abrupt or overwhelming. Here's how to ensure a smooth transition:

- **Assess Your Needs:** Before seeking professional help, understand what you need. Is it strategic direction, execution, or both? This will guide you in choosing the right type of marketing professional.
- **Research and Referrals:** Look for marketers with experience in your industry. Ask for referrals from your network, and check testimonials and case studies.
- **Marketing Expert vs. Virtual Assistant:** Consider whether you need a marketing expert to provide strategic guidance or a virtual assistant to handle

execution. Often, strategy should come before hiring someone for execution tasks.

- **Start with a Consultation:** Many marketers offer initial consultations. Use this opportunity to discuss your vision and see if their approach aligns with your goals.
- **Set Clear Expectations:** Once you decide to work with a professional, clearly work together to establish expectations, desired outcomes, and any concerns you may have.
- **Establish a Partnership:** Look for a marketer who is interested in a partnership rather than a transactional relationship. They should understand and respect your vision while guiding you with their expertise.
- **Regular Check-Ins:** Set up regular meetings to discuss progress, results, and adjustments. This keeps you in the loop and ensures that the marketing efforts are on track.
- **Evaluate and Adjust:** Regularly assess the impact of the professional's work on your business. Be open to making changes as needed to ensure that the marketing efforts are contributing to your business goals.

By recognizing when you need professional help and transitioning smoothly, you can ensure that your marketing efforts are effective, strategic, and aligned with your business's growth trajectory.

The Path to Marketing Maturity

The journey through (and past) the DIY marketing landscape is often fraught with hidden challenges and unexpected complexities. It's a path that many entrepreneurs embark upon with a sense of optimism, fueled by the promise of cost savings, control, and a personal touch. Yet, as we've explored, the reality is that marketing is a multifaceted discipline that requires specialized knowledge and experience to navigate successfully.

I always tell new entrepreneurs to **start wherever they need to start**, anywhere, doing anything … because most often in marketing anything is almost always better than nothing.

The limitations of a DIY approach may not be apparent to an entrepreneur immediately yet carry risks of oversimplification leading to costly mistakes. From SEO mishaps to misaligned marketing funnels, the potential for error is vast, as we've noted in some of the case studies already shared.

It's important to recognize that these challenges are not unique to you; they are part of a common narrative shared by many business owners striving to make their mark.

Seeking professional marketing help is not an admission of defeat; rather, it's an acknowledgment of the complexity of the marketing domain and a commitment to the growth and success of the future of your business.

As the CEO of your company, you should always strive to *hire people who are smarter than you*, and then let them do their job white you focus on your own Zone of Genius.

It's a step towards marketing maturity, where the insights and expertise of seasoned professionals can transform your marketing efforts from good to great.

Call to Action: Embrace Expertise

As you reflect on your marketing journey, consider the path you've taken and the direction in which you're headed.

- Are your efforts yielding the results you desire?
- Is the time you're investing in DIY marketing detracting from your core business activities?

If you find that your marketing strategy is not delivering the growth you seek, it may be time to embrace the expertise that professional guidance can offer.

Professional marketers bring a wealth of experience, strategic insight, and creative thinking to the table. They can help you avoid common pitfalls, refine your brand voice, and develop a strategy that aligns with your unique business goals. By partnering with a marketing expert, you can ensure that your marketing efforts are not just tasks to be completed, but strategic moves that contribute to your business's success.

Key Takeaways

- Recognize when to seek professional marketing help and understand the limitations of do-it-yourself approaches.

- Differentiate between tasks you can manage and those where expert assistance can significantly amplify your marketing efforts.

- Evaluate the cost-effectiveness of DIY strategies versus the potential ROI from professional marketing services.

- Understand the value of specialized skills and tools that professional marketers bring to your business.

The Fakexperts

The Fakexpert Phenomenon

Thanks to the accessibility of digital marketing, a new phenomenon, or menace, has emerged, who I've named the "Fakexpert." These are individuals who, emboldened by the anonymity and reach of the internet, claim a level of expertise they do not possess, at least not yet. They often lack the experience, results, or both, to back up their bold assertions.

The term itself is a portmanteau of 'fake' and 'expert', signifying someone who is masquerading as an authority in a field where they may have little more than a surface-level understanding. While I didn't create the word, I am claiming it for defining marketers who lack any expertise other than what they self-proclaim.

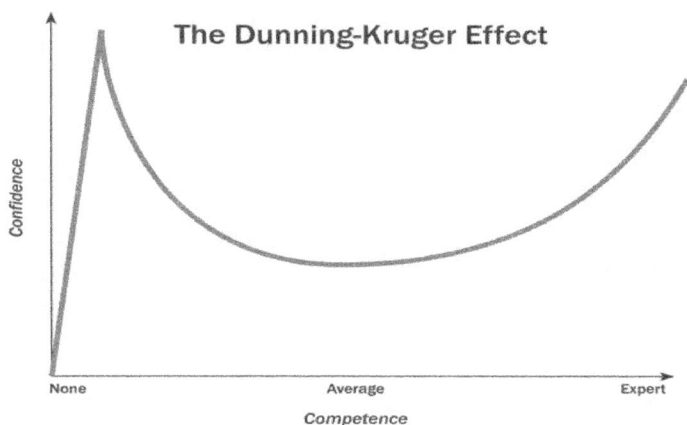

The Dunning-Kruger Effect

The Dunning-Kruger effect, a cognitive bias where individuals with limited knowledge or competence in a domain overestimate their own ability, often plays a role in the rise of Fakexperts. This phenomenon is well-documented, where it's clear that a little knowledge can be a dangerous thing, especially when it's wielded with unwarranted confidence.

The prevalence of Fakexperts in the marketing industry is **particularly troubling**. The low barrier to entry for online marketing platforms means that anyone with an internet connection can set up shop and start offering advice. The distinction between seasoned professionals and novices is crucial yet can be extremely hard to determine. True experts have a track record of success and can demonstrate their knowledge through results, not just rhetoric.

There can be many pitfalls of following guidance from Fakexperts. It's not uncommon for businesses to be led astray by strategies that sound promising but lack substance. This can lead to wasted resources, missed opportunities, and in some cases, significant setbacks for the business.

As we delve deeper into this phenomenon, we'll explore the characteristics of Fakexperts, learn how to spot them, and understand the impact they can have on businesses. The digital landscape is fertile ground for these individuals, but with the right knowledge and tools, businesses can learn to separate the wheat from the chaff and find marketing advice

that is not only sound but also tailored to their unique needs
and goals.

The Attraction of Quick Fixes and Big Promises

Entrepreneurs, by nature, are a breed of dreamers and
doers, often operating under tight constraints of time and
budget. This makes the siren call of quick fixes and big
promises almost irresistible. The allure lies in the hope of
immediate results and the dramatic success stories that
Fakexperts peddle. They promise a fast track to success, a
shortcut through the hard graft that building a business
typically requires. It's an attractive proposition: invest little,
reap much, and do it all at breakneck speed.

However, this attraction to apparently easy solutions is
fraught with peril. In the world of marketing, as in many
other fields, **if something sounds too good to be true, it
probably is**. The dangers of falling for such marketing are
manifold. First, these quick fixes often involve strategies that
are not sustainable in the long term. They might exploit a
loophole or trend that could disappear as quickly as it
emerged, leaving the business vulnerable and unprepared
for the aftermath.

Most often, these big promises fail to consider the unique
context of each business. What works for one company may
not work for another, and cookie-cutter solutions rarely
address the deeper challenges a business may face. The

result is a strategy that is misaligned with the company's goals, target audience, and brand identity, leading to ineffective marketing and wasted resources.

The biggest danger, perhaps, is the erosion of trust. When businesses are burned by Fakexperts, they become *wary of the marketing industry as a whole*. This skepticism can **close them off to genuine opportunities for growth**, as they become gun-shy about investing in legitimate marketing strategies in the future.

I see this every time that a new client comes to me who has been burned by a Fakexpert; they tend to question every recommendation initially *much more* than any other client we work with. I understand, so I answer, but there's a visible difference in the hesitation of these entrepreneurs, with good reason.

Entrepreneurs must be vigilant and discerning. It's essential to recognize that real success is rarely instantaneous and that effective marketing strategies require a deep understanding of the market, the audience, and the product or service being offered. By acknowledging this, businesses can avoid the pitfalls of empty promises and instead invest in solid, well-thought-out marketing plans that will yield sustainable growth and success over time.

Recognizing the Red Fakexpert Flags

In digital marketing where expertise is often self-proclaimed, it's crucial to discern the genuine from the counterfeit.

Recognizing the red flags can save you from the pitfalls of entrusting your marketing to a Fakexpert. Here are some warning signs to watch for:

- **Overpromising**: If someone guarantees overnight rankings, viral success, or other instantaneous results, be wary. Effective marketing and SEO are marathons, not sprints.
- **Lack of Proven Client Results:** A true expert will have a portfolio or case studies with measurable outcomes. If they can't show how their work has benefited other businesses, it's a red flag. Yet keep in mind even with published results, doesn't mean the results are real, nor that you can expect the same results.
- **Showing Only Their Own Results:** Unless you have exactly the same type of audience and sell exactly the same products or services, the "expert" showing you that they've made a million dollars this year doesn't mean you will. This is more akin to a Marketing MLM ... they'll teach you their process, which really only works for their business. Would you rather see that a marketer made a million bucks only for their own business, or that they helped numerous clients in numerous industries each make a million bucks?
- **One-Size-Fits-All Approach:** Marketing strategies should be bespoke and tailored for your business. If the approach seems generic or not customized to your market and audience, it's a sign of a Fakexpert.
- **Secretive or Vague Methods:** Transparency is key in marketing. If someone is secretive about their methods

or uses a lot of buzzwords without clear explanations, they may not have the expertise they claim.

- **No References or Testimonials:** Legitimate professionals will have clients who can vouch for their work. A lack of testimonials or references is concerning.
- **Cheap Services:** While everyone loves a good deal, extremely low prices can indicate that the services offered may not be thorough or of high quality. Sometimes it really is that you get what you pay for.
- **Pushy Sales Tactics:** High-pressure sales tactics can be a sign that the person is more interested in making a quick sale than in the long-term success of your marketing efforts. If a marketer is forcing you to make an immediate decision, this is a huge red flag. When I'm on the phone with someone and they say I only have until the end of the call, or two hours after the end of the call, or similar to decide, the answer is *always* no. The savviest entrepreneurs understand that other entrepreneurs often need to determine if a strategy is the right fit right now, and may need to do a bit of research. These pushy sales tactics only benefit the person selling, and like I always say, when you run across something that only benefits the person selling it to you, that's a red flag.
- **Lack of Industry Knowledge:** A true marketing expert will be up to date with the latest trends and algorithm

changes. If they seem out of touch with current marketing trends, it's a red flag.[12]

- **No Strategic Planning:** Fakexperts often jump straight into tactics without a strategic plan or learning about your uniqueness. Without a clear strategy, marketing efforts are less likely to succeed.
- **Ignoring Analytics:** If a marketer doesn't emphasize the importance of data and analytics, they're likely not equipped to measure and optimize campaign performance.

For example, a common red flag is the promise of "guaranteed" first-page search engine rankings. Search engines like Google frequently update their algorithms, and no one can guarantee specific ranking positions. If they are guaranteeing first position, it's paid ads, which is NOT SEO at all.

Another example is the recommendation to stuff keywords, an outdated and penalized practice that can harm your website's credibility and rankings. Yet I still see self-proclaimed SEO experts making this recommendation!

---

12 However, it's important not to dismiss advice simply because it differs from what you've previously heard. This is a common scenario for entrepreneurs who are transitioning from a startup phase to aiming for a million-dollar year. The strategies that got you here won't be the same as those needed to reach the next level. It's natural to question why the new advice sounds different, but it's essential to understand that your growth requires new approaches.

I've even had someone I was following on social media (as a way to support a fellow entrepreneur) who was a new copywriter, and after about 6 months in the business randomly decided they were suddenly now also an SEO expert. Amazing! It took me decades! She then told her followers to hide keywords on the page either in white text or behind some hidden elements on their page. This is BA BAD advice which can get your website *penalized by Google*. (And when I politely private-messaged her about how bad this advice is and that she might want to consider removing it from her posts, she blocked me. Yes, I know, shoot the messenger. Hope none of y'all are following her!)

And don't get distracted by lots of followers and engagement. There's one famous "marketer" who was consistently giving out bad advice that made me cringe *for years*. It was a case of accidental virality, not thoughtful strategies, and therefore no way it could work for everyone else. Only in the past couple of years are they finally saying things that now I think maybe they've learned basic marketing.

By being aware of these red flags, you can steer clear of Fakexperts and ensure that your marketing efforts are in the hands of someone who can truly help your business grow.

Case Study: The SEO Scam

Unfortunately, the story of a business ensnared by the false promises of a Fakexpert is all too common. This case study delves into the experience of a client who, seeking to enhance their online presence, fell victim to an SEO scam that promised much but delivered little.

The False Promises and Resulting Damage

Remember TeamSync Solutions? The business owner was not well-versed in the technicalities of SEO—just like most entrepreneurs are not—and was enticed by the promise of improved search engine rankings and handed over $2,500 a month to a freelancer who was claiming to be an SEO expert.

The first red flag was that the freelancer made a production version (or staging site) of the website public and indexed by Google, creating a duplicate content issue and competing with the live site for search engine rankings. Most staging sites are things that you never want the general public nor Google to see; it's where you test things which means that it's never finalized. Plus, it has a different address, which can cause all types of issues.

The second red flag arose when the freelancer focused on adding "transition words" to website content under the guise of SEO—a task that does little for search engine rankings nor, more importantly, for the reader. This entailed adding words like "Next", "However" or "Furthermore" to the beginning of sentences or paragraphs; an old recommendation that was never proven effective. As a case in point, would you have found this paragraph more compelling if I had added "Furthermore" as the first word? Nope.

The third, and perhaps most egregious red flag, was the freelancer's reckless handling of login credentials, granting excessive access to subcontractors (never agreed upon by the client) and risking the security and control of the client's website.

The Recovery Process

Upon realizing the freelancer's lack of knowledge (triggered when the company found out that the staging site was crawled and credentials were given out), TechSync Solutions owner sought genuine expertise to salvage their digital marketing efforts. I had worked with them in the past on another project, so they reached out to me to vet the recommendations and work this company was providing.

I must say, this freelancer wasn't necessarily a Fakexpert in all areas. He was an EXCELLENT salesman. He knew how to talk businesses into spending 4-figures a month on SEO. He knew NOTHING about SEO, just sold the service and then had a handful of people overseas who did whatever work they wanted. The people doing the work never spoke to the client. The salesman never spoke to the client about SEO (because he didn't know SEO). It was a weird setup that *didn't work for the client at all* (but worked great for the sales guy who was making $2,000 a month to sell and paying the other $500 a month to multiple overseas contractors),

The Recovery Process: A Detailed Look

The recovery process commenced with a meticulous audit of the website, to sift through the SEO work previously done. Here's what we uncovered and the steps we took to rectify the issues:

- **Duplicate Content Issues:** We discovered that the production version of the site was indexed by Google, creating duplicate content issues. Our immediate action was to:
    - Remove the production site from Google's index.
    - Implement proper use of the robots.txt file to prevent future indexing of any non-public domains.
- **Misguided "SEO Enhancements":** The freelancer's focus on adding transition words was misguided. We:
    - Reviewed and revised the content to ensure it was not just readable but also optimized for relevant keywords.
    - Eliminated unnecessary "fluff" additions that did not contribute to SEO or, more importantly, the reader (we *always* optimize for the reader first).
- **Access Control Negligence:** The freelancer had mishandled login credentials, compromising security. We:
    - Revoked unnecessary access permissions.
    - Established a secure protocol for credential management and subcontractor access.
- **Overlapping SEO Work:** Upon further investigation, we found that the client had over 50 websites, all competing

for the same keywords which diluted all SEO efforts. This was an old "grey hat" SEO practice that was now considered bad, which had been enacted by a different freelancer years before. To address this, we:

- Consolidated the websites, reducing the number from over 50 to less than 5 (only for different services).
- Redirected the traffic from the redundant sites to the main website to strengthen its SEO presence.

- **Content Strategy Overhaul:** The content across these multiple sites was not regularly updated, and when it was it lacked uniqueness with similar stories added to each site. We:

  - Developed a content calendar to ensure regular updates.
  - Created a strategy for unique content across the remaining sites to avoid penalties for duplicate content.

- **Social Media Confusion:** The client's social media strategy was scattered across too many profiles as well, leading to inconsistent messaging. We:

  - Consolidated social media profiles where possible.
  - Developed a cohesive social media strategy that aligned with the overall marketing goals.

- **Inefficient Processes:** The client was using a complex CRM system that was not sustainable for their size and was requiring a full-time team member to keep it running. This was the case of someone creating work to justify and keep their job. We:

- Recommended simplifying their CRM system to a managed solution that provided necessary support and integration.
- Streamlined their proposal process by integrating it into the CRM, eliminating the need for external Word documents.

- **Costly Redundancies:** The client was overpaying for services they didn't need, such as an expensive email provider despite never using all of the extra bells and whistles monthly. We:

  - Transitioned them to a more cost-effective email service provider that better suited their needs and offered automation capabilities.
  - Similarly, we found that they were also paying multiple freelancers for the same jobs, but without any coordination of efforts, so that work was always redundant. We made recommendations for streamlining this process, so that one focused on their portion of expertise, while the other was doing something different that fell under their own specialty.

As part of the full overview, we also found out that their earliest freelancer (who had set up the 50+ websites) was charging them monthly for pay-per-click ads. However, they were also paying Google directly for these same ads. And the freelancer had not touched the ad accounts in YEARS. So when they spent $1,000/month on their credit card paying

Google directly for these ads, the freelancer was also then billing them an extra $1,000 a month. For the same ads, which we had already edited and updated for them, with none of the original freelancer's work remaining. If you're saying WTF, so were we!

By addressing these specific issues, we were able to not only recover from the damage caused by the previous freelancers but also set the client on a path to sustainable and strategic SEO success.

The Outcome: By the Numbers

The transition from misguided guidance to a team equipped with genuine expertise and a strategic approach yielded tangible results for the client's business. Here's a breakdown of the outcomes in concrete numbers:

- **SEO and Organic Traffic:** After consolidating the websites, we saw a 75% increase in organic traffic within the first three months. This was a direct result of improved search engine rankings due to the elimination of duplicate content and a more focused keyword strategy.
- **Financial Savings:** By reducing the number of websites from over 50 to less than 5, the client saved approximately $15,000 annually in hosting, domain renewals, and associated maintenance costs. And then cutting off the duplication of paying for ad costs twice, saved them another $10,000 per year or so.

- **Operational Efficiency:** Streamlining the content management and social media strategy saved the client around 20 hours per week paid to freelancers. This equated to an annual saving of approximately 1,040 hours, which, when calculated against the average hourly rate for a marketing manager, translated to a cost saving of around $52,000.

- **Increased Revenue:** With a more robust online presence and improved SEO, the client reported a revenue increase of $42,000 in the first month post-implementation of the new strategies.

- **Cost Reduction in Email Marketing:** By switching to a more cost-effective email service provider, the client saved $2,100 annually while gaining additional automation features that saved several hours of manual work each month.

- **CRM System Simplification:** The recommendation to simplify their CRM system potentially saved the client from having a full-time programmer, which usually costs upwards of $50,000 per year for the least expensive programmers. While they did move from a self-hosted (free) version of the CRM to a cloud-based version managed by the company, the added cost for the subscription of $1,200 per year was more than offset by the cost savings of not requiring a full-time programmer dedicated only to this one software. Additionally, the new system reduced downtime and inefficiencies, although exact numbers for these savings are harder to quantify without further ongoing detailed analysis.

I'm not sure if you're doing the math here … we saved them roughly $125,000 in a year and helped them increase their income roughly $400,000 at the same time.

But let's look at the Beyond-the-Graph Growth™. The client's journey from the pitfalls of quick-fix SEO to a sustainable, well-informed strategy not only saved them money and time but also provided a solid foundation for future growth.

This case study highlights the critical importance of vetting the expertise of marketing professionals, understanding the basics of the services being contracted, and ensuring that there is a clear and transparent line of communication throughout the process. It's a testament to the fact that in marketing, shortcuts can lead to long-term setbacks, and investing in genuine expertise pays dividends.

The Cost of Misplaced Trust

When a business places its trust in a so-called expert, it's not just investing money; it's investing hope, time, and their very reputation. The allure of a Fakexpert often lies in their confident promises of rapid results and cost savings, but the reality is that the true cost of this misplaced trust can be staggering.

Financial Costs:

The most immediate and measurable impact of following a Fakexpert's advice is financial. Businesses may find themselves locked into costly contracts, paying for services that are at best ineffective and at worst harmful to their digital presence, as the case study already showcased.

For instance, a business might spend thousands on black-hat SEO tactics in the past that ultimately lead to Google penalties, or on social media strategies that do nothing to engage their actual customer base. The cost of these services is just the tip of the iceberg; the real financial hit comes when you factor in the opportunity cost of lost leads, sales, and the potential revenue that could have been generated with effective marketing strategies.

Operational Costs:

Operational inefficiency is another hidden cost. Misguided strategies can lead to a significant waste of time—both in the implementation of ineffective tactics and in the eventual need to correct them. This time could have been spent on productive, revenue-generating activities.

The internal resources spent managing these inefficiencies can lead to burnout and turnover, which carry their own costs in terms of recruitment, training, and lost institutional knowledge.

Reputational Costs:

Perhaps the most insidious cost of all is the damage to a company's reputation. In the digital age, trust is currency, and once it's lost, it's incredibly difficult to regain. A Fakexpert's strategies may not only fail to engage the right audience but could actively alienate a business's core customer base.

For example, aggressive email marketing tactics can lead to brand fatigue and a tarnished reputation, while poor-quality content can diminish a brand's perceived expertise and authority in its field. I was speaking to a business recently that was adding people to their email audience using a strategy that, while *technically* had them opting in, it wasn't overly apparent to them that they were doing so. This can damage a company's reputation.

Long-Term Impact:

The long-term impact of these costs can be profound. Financial losses can restrict a business's ability to invest in genuine growth opportunities. Operational inefficiencies can lead to a culture of short-term thinking and a lack of strategic focus. And a tarnished reputation can have a chilling effect on customer acquisition and retention, supplier relationships, and even the ability to attract top talent.

The true cost of following a Fakexpert's advice is not just in the immediate resources wasted but in the ripple effect of those decisions. It can set a business back by months or even years, undermining its competitive position and its ability to achieve sustainable growth.

The path to recovery often requires not only financial investment to correct course but also a concerted effort to rebuild trust and operational stability. It's a stark reminder that when it comes to marketing expertise, if it sounds too good to be true, it probably is.

Building a Defense Against Fakexperts

It's crucial for businesses to build a robust defense against Fakexperts. This defense begins with a thorough vetting process for any potential marketing partners or advisors. Here are strategies to ensure you're engaging with genuine expertise:

Research and Reviews:

Start with due diligence. Research the individual or agency online.

When together with the client we did a quick Google Search of the freelancer (aka salesman) he hired, we found that the self-proclaimed SEO expert could only be found online *in one spot*—as a salesman for car parts. An SEO expert who can't be found online when you search their exact name. Red flag that they can't effectively do their own SEO.

Consider their online presence: do they have a website? Does their website showcase their expertise?

It can be challenging to assess expertise in unfamiliar fields, but here's an example for perspective. On my website, you'll find around 400 articles related to different aspects of marketing, with new insights added regularly. This is a testament to my commitment to both gaining and sharing expertise. While the sheer volume of content alone can't define expertise, it can be a useful indicator. For instance, compare this to another marketing professional whose business has been open a similar amount of time but with only a single, superficial article on their site. This contrast could highlight a significant difference in expertise and dedication to the field.

Also look for reviews, testimonials, and case studies. Reviews or testimonials should be on their website and may also be found on third-party sites like Google, LinkedIn, and industry-specific platforms when it makes sense, and can provide a well-rounded view of their reputation. While online reviews can be easier to fake (we've all heard stories about businesses who get slammed with a ton of negative reviews from friends of someone who felt somehow slighted), case studies can provide more detail with examples of the types of services provided and results that their clients experienced. (But make sure that those aren't what we see in the case of many MLMs … a testimonial or case study that had results from one pro, and now all of the fakexperts beneath them use that same one case study, even though they're not the ones who created the results. Like the photo of "Andrea" with her before and after weight loss … but it was someone completely different on another arm of the MLM who helped "Andrea" get her results 10 years ago, and now her same photos are used with a different name by 1,000 other sellers. Sorry … it's a pet peeve of mine and I'll get off my soapbox now.)

Yet don't let quantity of these items alone sway you. I usually only request a review at the point when a project is complete, and since many of our clients have ongoing services, I may not have requested one yet (yes, I know, I need to change this lol). I'm also the world's worst at creating and finishing case studies (a project that I probably need to hand off to someone on my own team!) There's also plenty of bad actors who simply pay for some questionable service that will post tons of fake reviews (good for you, or negative for a competitor. Bad practice!).

But lacking *any* of this would be a big red flag.

Ask for References:

A genuine expert should be able to provide references from past clients. Don't just ask for the references, follow up with them. Ask these clients about their results, their working relationship with the expert, and whether they felt they got value for their investment.

Examine Case Studies:

Request detailed case studies that include not just narratives but data and outcomes (which is why I always try to include the numbers in the ones I create - that's important stuff!). Look for evidence of sustained success, not just quick wins. You're not looking for samples of the work per se (except maybe if you're needing graphic design and want to see other designs by the same artist), but results. Be wary of any "expert" who cannot provide concrete examples of their work or only provides fluff.

Evaluate Their Content:

Look at the content they've produced. Is it insightful, accurate, and up to date? A true expert will share knowledge freely, contributing to blogs, webinars, and industry discussions. It's not about quantity; their thought leadership can be a reflection of their depth of understanding.

Probe Their Knowledge:

When you meet (whether in person or virtually), ask probing questions. Don't just ask about their successes; ask about challenges they've faced and how they've overcome them. Inquire about their approach to changes in the industry and how they stay current with best practices.

Look for a Holistic, Bespoke Approach:

Be cautious of anyone who promises quick fixes using their system. Genuine experts understand that digital marketing is a complex, evolving discipline that requires a holistic approach. They should be talking about strategy, not just tactics.

Transparency and Reporting:

Ask about their reporting methods. They should be able to explain how they measure success and be willing to share those metrics with you regularly (for example, any client who has multiple months of work, or ongoing services, we set up a dashboard that the client can access at any time). Transparency is key.

Beware of Guarantees:

Steer clear of anyone who guarantees specific results, especially within a short time frame. In marketing, there are no guarantees, only strategies that increase the likelihood of success. It's still you and your business that needs to drive the final leg of outcomes. Unless the marketer is doing 100% of all marketing work, which includes strategy around product, price, placement, people, the sales process, and more than simply promoting what you're selling, they don't have full control over all of the results; and if they don't realize this fact, it's a red flag.

Trust Your Instincts:

Finally, trust your instincts. If something feels off during your interactions, or if the expert seems more focused on closing a sale than understanding your business, it may be a sign to walk away. You need to feel like you can build a long-term relationship with the person or company that you're speaking to, even if you only have one project right now. It has to feel good, with confidence that you'll be able to work together.

By incorporating these strategies into your vetting process, you can significantly reduce the risk of engaging with a Fakexpert. Remember, the goal is to find a partner who will work with you to achieve sustainable growth, not someone who offers a dazzling presentation without the substance to back it up.

The Value of True Expertise

The distinction between real and fake experts is not just a matter of wasted dollars—it's about the trajectory of your business. True expertise in marketing is an amalgamation of experience, ongoing education, and a proven track record. It's about transparency in methods and communication, showcasing a history of success, and the humility to adapt strategies to the unique contours of each business's needs and market dynamics.

The value of genuine expertise cannot be overstated. Real experts don't just bring results; they bring sustainability and growth. They understand the nuances of consumer behavior, the intricacies of various digital platforms, and the importance of aligning marketing strategies with business objectives. Their strategies are not one-size-fits-all but are as unique as the businesses they serve. They are partners in growth, not just service providers.

Well, Vicky ... I Hired a Fakexpert and Got Poor Results, What Do I Do Now?

1. **Recognize the Misstep**: Recognize that hiring a 'Fakexpert' was a misstep. Understanding and accepting this is the first step towards making a better choice next time.

124

2. **Analyze What Went Wrong**: Reflect on why the results were poor. Was it a lack of expertise, misaligned strategies, or unrealistic expectations?

3. **Reassess Your Needs**: Take a step back and reassess your business's marketing needs. Clearly define what you are looking for in a marketing expert or strategy.

4. **Learn from the Experience**: Use this experience to sharpen your ability to discern genuine expertise in the future. Look for signs of proven experience, testimonials, and a deep understanding of your specific market.

5. **Pivot with a Clear Plan**: Develop a new plan that addresses the shortcomings of the previous approach. This might involve setting clearer goals, connecting with a marketing expert, or taking time to educate yourself more on marketing fundamentals (not so that you can do the work, but so that you can supervise if needed).

6. **Implement and Monitor**: Carefully implement your new strategy with the right expert or approach. Closely monitor the results and be ready to make adjustments as needed.

Call to Action: Due Diligence in Expert Selection

Before you place the future of your business's online presence in the hands of a marketing professional, pause and perform thorough due diligence. Your business deserves the best, and that means taking the time to ensure you're partnering with a true expert.

Here's a checklist to guide you through the process:

Marketing Professional Credibility Checklist:

- ☐ **Experience and Results:** Look for a portfolio of work that demonstrates a breadth of experience and tangible results.
- ☐ **Testimonials and References:** Seek out feedback from previous clients to gauge satisfaction and impact.
- ☐ **Content Contribution:** Evaluate the quality and insight of their published work, including articles, blogs, and speaking engagements.
- ☐ **Strategic Approach:** Ensure they have a strategic, not just tactical, approach to marketing.
- ☐ **Transparency:** Confirm that they offer clear reporting and open communication channels.
- ☐ **Adaptability:** Check that they tailor strategies to fit different business models and objectives.
- ☐ **Ethical Practices:** Ascertain that they adhere to ethical practices in marketing.
- ☐ **No Unrealistic Promises:** Be wary of guarantees that seem too good to be true.
- ☐ **Personal Rapport:** Trust your instincts about their professionalism and passion for marketing.

Use this checklist as a starting point in your search for a marketing expert. Remember, the right partnership can elevate your business to new heights. Take the time, ask the tough questions, and choose a path of growth backed by true expertise. Your business's future is worth that investment.

Key Takeaways

- Learn to differentiate between genuine marketing expertise and misleading advice.

- Develop a critical eye for evaluating the credibility and track record of marketing 'experts.'

- Seek advice that aligns with your business values and goals, rather than flashy, one-size-fits-all promises.

- Focus on building a network of trusted and proven marketing professionals for reliable guidance.

Part II: Focusing on the Wrong Numbers

In the second chapter of our expedition, we delve into the numbers game—a domain where many entrepreneurs *mistakenly equate* **activity** with **accomplishment**. This segment is about discerning the *meaningful metrics* from the *misleading ones* and understanding that the true measure of marketing success goes beyond surface-level statistics.

The Mirage of Metrics

In the dense forest of data, it's easy to chase after the allure of impressive numbers. Social media likes, shares, and comments can feel like a pat on the back, but do they translate to genuine business growth? We'll venture into the deceptive world of vanity metrics to uncover the truth behind the numbers. Through the lens of a business that once mistook 'likes' for leads, we'll learn to align our compass to the metrics that truly map our progress.

The Alchemy of Allocation

The art of allocation is akin to a tightrope walk above the chasm of financial uncertainty. How do you distribute your limited resources for maximum impact? This section dispels the fog of financial fear, guiding you through the principles of prudent budgeting and resource allocation. Witness the transformation of a business that learned to invest not just money, but faith in a marketing budget tailored to their unique journey.

The Data Detour

In the quest for knowledge, it's tempting to collect every scrap of data, but not all information is a treasure—some is just trivia. Here, we'll learn to sidestep the data detour, focusing on the metrics that merit our attention. By examining the pitfalls of data overload and the liberation of data discernment, we'll equip ourselves with the savvy to separate the wheat from the chaff.

In Part II, you'll gain the insight to navigate the numerical nuances of marketing.

What's in it for you? A clear-eyed view of your business landscape, the ability to allocate your assets astutely, and the foresight to follow the figures that truly forecast your future success.

Let's turn the page on the superficial and steer towards the substantial.

The Mirage of Metrics

Navigating Metrics and Analytics

Metrics and analytics are the constellations by which savvy entrepreneurs chart their course in the vast ocean of marketing. The landscape is dotted with an almost infinite array of data points: from page views and click-through rates to engagement metrics and conversion percentages. It's a cosmos where numbers reign supreme, but not all numbers wield the same power or tell the truth about the health and trajectory of a business.

The common misconception that *more activity is always better* can lead many astray in this complex metric terrain.

I first realized this activity fallacy in high school, when I was Editor of the school newspaper and yearbook my senior year. As Editor, I was the one who handed out assignments to the rest of the "staff" of journalists and photographers and made sure that whatever important events and newsworthy stories were properly covered.

Working with a small team that year, there were a handful of us who had fairly free reign, with nearly half of our day spent running the publications. (You know how by senior year you tend to get more electives, and three of mine were Yearbook class). During this time, we had our "staff" passes to be able to go around the school as needed to get our work done. Something came up needing a photographer, and as I was going into the school office I saw our head photographer walking out. I said Hey (insert name here), I need you to go take a photo of … whatever it was going on at that point, the activity isn't nearly as important as the lesson. He said, "I can't, I'm too busy." The school period he was in the yearbook class, I was over assignments in that class (with the teacher, of course), I had not given him an assignment, and he did not have his camera. I asked, "doing what?" to which he replied, 'just busy' as he was out the door.

And I learned … activity does not equal results. (Yes, we had a chat later.)

A high number of page views or a surge in social media followers might seem like a clear signal of success, but these metrics can be misleading if they don't translate into **tangible business outcomes**. The allure of these 'vanity metrics'—those impressive-looking numbers that, upon closer inspection, hold little value in driving strategic decisions—can cause even the most astute entrepreneurs to lose their way.

You have 10,000 followers? 10,000,000 followers? How much profit are they making you … that's the question when you're running a business.

Metrics serve a critical role in marketing strategy, acting as the compass that guides business decisions. When used correctly, they provide invaluable insights into customer behavior, campaign performance, and return on investment. They help entrepreneurs to understand not just the 'what' of customer actions, but the 'why' behind them. This understanding allows for the fine-tuning of strategies, the optimization of campaigns, and, ultimately, the growth of the business.

To harness the true power of metrics, you must first understand their purpose. They are not just numbers to be increased for their own sake, but signposts that point toward deeper insights and strategic opportunities. They should inform and influence actions, prompting entrepreneurs to ask questions like:

- Which channels are most effective at reaching our target audience?
- What type of content resonates best with our customers?
- How can we improve the customer journey to increase conversions and customer satisfaction?

By focusing on metrics that align with business goals, you can move beyond the superficial and develop strategies that drive real, sustainable growth. It's about quality over quantity, relevance over reach, and impact over impressions. With a clear understanding of the landscape and the purpose of metrics, businesses can navigate the complex world of digital marketing with confidence and precision.

Remember, your most important metric is always profit (not necessarily revenue).

The Vanity of Social Media Metrics

'Likes' and 'shares' can sound like applause to the ears of entrepreneurs. And we have been trained by social media platforms to respond to those like Pavlov's dogs responded salivating at the bell.

Social media platforms have become stages where businesses perform daily, and each reaction can feel like a standing ovation. Every thumbs up feels like validation that sometimes entrepreneurs really need to hear.

Yet, these metrics, as intoxicating as they may be, are often misleading indicators of success. They are the vanity metrics: attractive, sometimes ego-stroking, but not necessarily reflective of a business's health or growth.

The Allure of Likes and Shares

The immediate gratification of watching 'likes' tick upwards can be alluring. It's a quick hit of dopamine that suggests approval and acceptance. But what do these metrics actually mean for your business? A 'like' is an ambiguous nod of acknowledgment; a 'share' might extend your reach, but does it convert to sales or lead to meaningful engagement with your brand? Do they at least increase lasting awareness?

The answer is not always clear. These metrics are often just the surface sheen, a facade that can distract from the foundational aspects of business growth.

Beyond the Applause

To truly measure the impact of social media efforts, we must look past the applause and towards the metrics that matter: things like (depending upon your unique needs and goals) conversion rates, website traffic, lead generation, and ultimately, sales into profits.

Just because someone engages with a post on social media, does not mean that they will EVER make a purchase. They may be the wrong audience but like what you posted. They may appear to be the right audience but not have the money or the desire to spend the money (which would make them the wrong audience).

Conversions are the indicators that your content is not just seen but is **compelling enough to inspire action**. They tell you whether your social media presence is a mere spectacle or a powerful engine driving growth.

Case Study: A Cautionary Tale from Facebook

Consider the case of the owner of a business we will call Bubbles & Bliss, who ran a thriving six-figure business selling hand-crafted soaps and related products exclusively through Facebook. With no website to call her own, she placed her entire digital existence in the hands of a third-party platform - Facebook. That's what her Fakexpert "coach" told her to do.

It was a risky move that many don't consider until it's too late. Her Facebook page had turned into a bustling marketplace, filled with customer interactions, ongoing projects, and a steady stream of 'likes' and 'shares' that seemed to validate her business model considering she would also get sales.

However, the entrepreneur's reliance on Facebook proved to be her undoing when, without warning, the platform shut down her page. (Oh, the woes of so many entrepreneurs who this has happened to, either temporarily or permanently!) The reasons for such drastic action can range from algorithmic errors to policy changes, but the result is the same: immediate and total loss of access to customers, ongoing projects, and all accumulated business data.

This entrepreneur's experience mirrors a similar story I detailed on my podcast, where a 6-figure Etsy seller faced the abrupt closure of her store. With no ability to appeal, she was left adrift, severed from her customer base with no means of contact. It took her nearly two years to rebuild what was lost in an instant—a sobering reminder of the perils of platform dependency when it's the platform that owns all parts of our existence.

The lesson here is stark: **third-party sites wield full control over your content and your access to customers.** Building your business on this type of rented land is a gamble that can cost you dearly.

While social media can be a powerful tool for engagement and brand awareness, it should not be the sole repository for your digital presence. Diversify your platforms, establish your own domain, and ensure that you have direct lines of communication with your customers.

Only then can you protect your business from the capricious whims of third-party platforms and build a resilient, sustainable digital foundation.

Case Study: A Cautionary Tale from TikTok

Another cautionary tale emerges from TikTok. I once worked with a client we will call HarmonyTech, who had established a robust following on the platform and their TikTok presence was driving substantial traffic to their website, funneling a handful of visitors to purchase their services.

On the surface, this strategy appeared effective, but it demanded an immense amount of direct effort from the CEO. TikTok, while a social media platform, requires a unique approach. Unlike other platforms where content might continue to generate engagement even during brief hiatuses, TikTok operates differently. It's akin to paid advertising in its immediacy and need for constant input; the moment you stop posting, its efficacy dwindles. This intensive demand on the CEO's time was proving unsustainable.

The CEO's commitment to TikTok, while impressive in driving substantial website traffic, was ultimately unsustainable. His proficiency in leveraging the platform might have seemed like his 'zone of genius,' but it wasn't the most strategic focus for the business's long-term health.

Another problem, while it could drive traffic, a sizable portion of the traffic consisted of casual browsers (tire kickers) unlikely to convert into customers ever, and another group of potential buyers often not ready to commit until much later. This situation highlighted a gap in creating 'microconversions,' such as capturing email addresses for ongoing engagement.

The unsustainability of TikTok was proven when he pivoted to focus on some other areas of the business, and traffic dried up when his posting did. We came in and began layering in other, more sustainable strategies to their marketing mix. These strategies required time and consistency to flourish, but they were crucial in building a robust, sustainable foundation for the business's future growth and could work as a great complement to existing strategies while the pivot was made from TikTok to everything else.

These two case studies underscore a vital lesson: the importance of marketing diversification. Relying heavily on a single platform, especially one as volatile as TikTok, or that seems to enjoy banning folks like Facebook, is a risky game. You need a strategy that both works now and that you can build upon later for longevity and stability, aligning more closely with their long-term business goals.

Oh No, Vicky... a Third Party Platform is my Primary Place, What Should I Do?

Understanding the Challenge: Recognize that while social media can be a powerful tool, over-reliance on any single platform, especially volatile ones like Facebook or TikTok, or even Etsy as we've seen in the case of one of my clients, can be risky. It's crucial to diversify your marketing strategies for stability and longevity.

Pivoting to Diversification:

1. **Expand Your Marketing Channels**: Start exploring other marketing avenues like email marketing, content marketing, SEO, and paid ads to reduce over-dependence on social media.
2. **Focus on Building Relationships**: Use social media to create initial connections, but then deepen those relationships through more direct and personalized channels, and get these connections OFF your social media and into your own platform (email, web, etc.)
3. **Leverage Data Wisely**: Collect data from your social media interactions but use it to inform broader marketing strategies that go beyond social platforms.
4. **Sustainable Content Strategies**: Develop content strategies that work across multiple platforms, ensuring

your efforts continue to pay off even if you scale back on social media.

5. **Long-term Planning**: Align your marketing efforts with long-term business goals, ensuring each tactic contributes to a bigger picture.

Adapting for Sustainability: Realize that a successful pivot involves not just adding new channels, but also optimizing and aligning them with your business's overall growth strategy.

The Sanity of Sales-Driven Data

I'm a huge fan of the data that we can get from our marketing efforts which was never traditionally available before, yet there's SO MUCH data that it's easy to lose your way.

There is a compass that reliably points to true north: sales and conversion data. These metrics cut through the noise and show the real impact of marketing efforts on the bottom line. They are the sanity in a world often distracted by vanity metrics.

Sales Metrics as True North

Sales metrics are the heartbeat of a business, the most honest indicators of its health and vitality. While likes and shares are the echoes of potential interest, sales and conversions are the sound of commitment—a customer's decision to invest in what you offer. These metrics provide the most direct correlation to your marketing strategies, offering clear insights into what works and what doesn't.

Interpreting Sales Data

Understanding sales data goes beyond tallying transactions; it's about interpreting the story behind the numbers.

- Which products are bestsellers, and why?
- What times of year do you see a spike in purchases, and how can you capitalize on that seasonality?
- How do customer behaviors on your website lead to a sale, and at what point do you lose them?

Analyzing sales data allows you to refine your marketing approach, target your efforts more effectively, and allocate resources to the strategies that yield the best return on investment. It's about connecting each sale to the marketing activity that drove it and using that knowledge to drive future campaigns.

Case Study: A Success Story of Sales-Driven Strategy

Let's turn our attention to a case study that exemplifies the power of a sales-driven data approach. A mid-sized e-commerce company that we will call GreenLeaf Outdoor Gear was struggling with stagnant sales despite a high volume of traffic from their social media channels. They had been focusing on engagement metrics but found that these did not translate into increased revenue.

The shift came when we helped GreenLeaf start to track the journey of social media traffic through to their website and, ultimately, to the checkout. They implemented tracking codes (which can be easy to do with simple UTM tags) to understand which social media posts were not just popular, but which were profitable.

This led to a revelation: the posts that were driving actual sales *were not the ones with the most likes or comments*, but those that provided in-depth product information such as showing how to use a particular item, and customer testimonials.

Armed with this insight, the company restructured their social media strategy to focus on content that guided potential customers through the sales funnel. Even if those posts didn't achieve many likes. They invested in more photography and video, detailed descriptions, and leveraged customer feedback as social proof.

The results were clear and measurable. Within six months, GreenLeaf saw a 50% increase in sales originating from social media, and combined with some other strategies we helped implement, a significant uptick in average order value, and a reduction in cart abandonment rates. By anchoring their strategy in **sales-driven data**, they were able to cut through the clutter and invest in marketing that delivered tangible results.

This success underscores the importance of sales metrics as the guiding star for marketing efforts. It's a testament to the fact that when you align your marketing compass to sales-driven data, you navigate your business towards true growth and sustainability.

Interpreting Your Marketing Metrics

Navigating the sea of analytics reports can be daunting. The key is not just to collect data, but to decode it—to read between the lines and understand the story it tells about your business and your customers.

Decoding Data

To truly interpret your marketing metrics, you need to look beyond the surface. It's not just about how many people visited your site, but how they interacted with it. Did they bounce off the homepage, or did they engage further with your content? Which pages held their attention, and which ones didn't? Are there spots better at driving sales?

For example, a high number of page views on your website might seem positive, but if those views have a high bounce rate, it could indicate that the content isn't resonating with your audience or that the page isn't user-friendly. Yet it could also mean that your prospect found exactly what they needed (at this time) on this page, and if you have a longer sales cycle timeline, they may be back for more later. If that's the case, you'll want to add a way that you can create a microconversion.

On the other hand, if you have a lower number of page views but those visitors are spending time on your site and engaging with your content, that's usually a sign of a more interested and invested audience. Yet if they never get to a sale, you could still have an issue.

Actionable Insights

The goal is to turn these insights into actions. If certain pages have high engagement, analyze what they have in common and replicate those elements across your site. If a particular source of traffic is leading to more conversions, invest more in that channel.

For instance, if you find that visitors from your email newsletter spend more time on your site and have a higher conversion rate than those from social media, this might prompt you to focus more on growing your email list and creating more targeted content for that audience.

Marketing Mirror

Have you ever focused on a metric that, in hindsight, wasn't so crucial to your business success? What was it?

_____

_____

How do you determine which metrics are most important to your marketing goals?

_____

_____

Business Goals

Note a few of your overall business goals, and then note a metric that could provide data as to whether or not you're reaching your goal. I've started you off with a couple.

Goal	Metric
Increase revenue	Monthly sales numbers
Increase website traffic	Google Analytics traffic
Increase awareness	Social media engagement

Measuring Marketing Success

Success in marketing is not a one-size-fits-all metric. It's a personalized story that aligns with your business goals and growth trajectory.

Defining Success

Success might look like increased brand awareness, a higher conversion rate, or improved customer retention. It's essential to define what success means for your business and then measure your marketing efforts against that standard.

As an example, if your goal is to increase brand awareness, you might track metrics like social media reach, brand mentions, and media coverage. If your goal is to improve sales, you'll focus on conversion rates, average order value, and customer lifetime value.

The Right Tools

To track and analyze these metrics effectively, you need the right tools. Google Analytics is a powerful tool for understanding website traffic and user behavior. Social media analytics can provide insights into your audience's engagement and demographics. CRM software can help you track sales, customer interactions, and the effectiveness of your sales funnel.

Each tool provides a piece of the puzzle. By using them in tandem, you can get a comprehensive view of your marketing performance and make informed decisions about where to allocate your resources for the maximum impact.

One of the mistakes I have seen is an entrepreneur switching up the services they use to track metrics so often, that they can't compare apples to apples. This included one company that changed their Google Analytics tag every time a new person refreshed their website. Instead of having years and years of historical data, they tended to only have access to about six months' worth at any one time. That data is nearly useless! (We helped them fix this problem by making sure that THEY owned the analytics account, and their vendors were invited to use it, therefore allowing them to keep the same tracking tag).

By interpreting your marketing metrics correctly and measuring your success against the right standards, you can ensure that your marketing efforts are not just busy work, but strategic moves that drive your business forward.

The Mirage Revealed

As we pull back the curtain on the metrics mirage, we find that the true value lies not in the volume of data, but in the insights that data can provide. It's about understanding the story behind the numbers and making informed decisions that align with your business goals.

Throughout this portion of our exploration, we've uncovered the pitfalls of vanity metrics and the allure of likes and shares. We've seen how they can distract from the metrics that truly indicate business growth and success. We've learned that sales and conversion data are the compass that guides us to our true north—profitable and sustainable business growth.

We've also delved into the art of interpreting marketing metrics, emphasizing the need to decode the data to extract actionable insights. It's not just about collecting analytics; it's about understanding what they mean for your business and how you can use them to make strategic decisions.

Call to Action: Connecting Data to Goals

Now, it's time to apply these lessons to your own marketing practices. Begin by revisiting your marketing goals and the metrics you currently track. Are they aligned? Do they provide you with the insights you need to make informed decisions?

Here's a checklist to help you focus on the metrics that might matter:

- **Define Your Success Metrics:** Align your metrics with your business objectives. Whether it's brand awareness, lead generation, or customer retention, ensure your metrics reflect these goals.
- **Look Beyond Surface-Level Data:** Don't get caught up in numbers that look good on paper but don't contribute to your bottom line. Focus on metrics that show engagement and conversion.
- **Use the Right Tools:** Equip yourself with the proper analytics tools that can help you track and interpret your data effectively.
- **Regularly Review Your Data:** Make data review a regular part of your routine. This will help you stay on top of trends and make timely adjustments to your strategy.
- **Test and Optimize:** Use A/B testing to find out what works best for your audience and continuously optimize your marketing efforts based on your findings.

- **Educate Your Team:** Ensure everyone involved understands which metrics are important and why. This will help align efforts across your organization.
- **Stay Agile:** Be prepared to pivot your strategy based on what your data is telling you. The digital landscape is always changing, and so should your approach.

By focusing on the metrics that truly matter, you can peel away the layers of illusion and reveal the core of your marketing effectiveness. This clarity will not only save you time and resources but will also propel your business towards real, measurable growth.

Take these insights, apply them with diligence, and watch as the mirage of misleading metrics fades to reveal the oasis of actionable, meaningful data that can lead to your business's success.

Key Takeaways

- Focus on the data that truly matters and avoid being misled by irrelevant metrics.

- Identify key performance indicators (KPIs) that directly impact your business goals.

- Avoid over-reliance on vanity metrics and concentrate on actionable insights that drive growth.

- Regularly review and adjust your metrics strategy to align with evolving business objectives.

The Alchemy of Allocation

The distribution of business resources is not just a matter of numbers; it's an alchemical process that transforms raw inputs into golden opportunities. This section will guide you through the mystical art of budgeting and resource allocation, turning the mundane into the magical.

Fundamentals of Budgeting and Resource Allocation

The Budgeting Mindset

To embark on the financial portion of your marketing journey, you must first adopt the right mindset. Budgeting, in its essence, is not about constraints; it's a strategic exercise that empowers you to allocate your resources in alignment with your most critical business goals. It's about making choices that can propel your business forward and turning the lead of limited resources into the gold of lucrative returns.

The Foundation of Financial Planning

A well-planned budget is the cornerstone of any successful marketing strategy. It's the foundation upon which the health of your business rests. A budget that is both realistic and flexible serves as a roadmap, guiding your spending in directions that are most likely to yield returns. It ensures that every dollar you invest is working towards the growth and sustainability of your business.

In marketing, where the temptation to chase after the latest trends can be strong, a solid budget acts as a grounding force. It helps you to prioritize initiatives that align with your business objectives and to avoid the pitfalls of impulsive spending on unproven tactics. The one thing that forced me to be the most strategic about where, when and how I allocated my own marketing dollars was when I was entirely bootstrapping my business.

A budget also provides a framework for measuring the effectiveness of your marketing efforts. By setting clear financial parameters, you can better assess which strategies are delivering value and which are not. This clarity allows for more informed decision-making and strategic adjustments as needed.

In the next sections, we will explore how to craft a budget that reflects your business's unique needs and goals, how to allocate resources wisely, and how to adjust your spending in response to the ever-evolving landscape of the market. The goal is to ensure that every resource you allocate is an *investment* in your business's future, not just an *expense*.

Budgeting Without Breaking

Creating a marketing budget that supports your business goals without overextending your resources is akin to performing a perfectly balanced ballet. It requires poise,

154

precision, and an understanding of the core principles that govern prudent budgeting.

One of the most frequent questions I get is, "**how much should my budget be?**" While there's no universal figure, a general guideline suggests allocating about 20% of your revenue to marketing. This percentage will fluctuate depending on your business's growth stage; early startups may need more. Keep this rough estimate in mind as you work through the upcoming sections, particularly if you're still in the early stages of budget planning.

Principles of Prudent Budgeting

The first step in prudent budgeting is to recognize that not all marketing efforts require massive investments to be effective. The key is to focus on strategies that offer the highest return on investment (ROI) and to leverage cost-effective methods that can yield substantial results. Here are some principles to guide you:

- **Prioritize High-ROI Activities:** Concentrate on marketing activities that have historically provided the best returns. This could mean refining your email marketing campaigns, optimizing your website for search engines, or engaging with customers on social media. I discuss this a bit in our 3x3 Marketing Matrix™ that I will introduce later.
- **Lean on Analytics:** Use data analytics to understand where your previous marketing efforts have succeeded

and where they haven't. This will help you make informed decisions about where to allocate your budget.

- **Be Agile:** The digital landscape is ever-changing. Your budget should be flexible enough to allow for shifts in strategy when certain channels or tactics prove to be more effective than others.
- **Test and Scale:** Start with small tests for new marketing strategies to gauge their effectiveness. If they perform well, then you can confidently scale up your investment.
- **Consider the Long-Term:** Some marketing strategies may take longer to pay off. Allocate a portion of your budget to these long-term investments while balancing them with short-term wins.

Adapting to Business Size and Stage

The size of your business and its stage of growth are critical factors in determining how to allocate your marketing budget. A startup might focus on brand awareness and customer acquisition, while an established company might invest more in customer retention and upselling.

- **For Startups:** Budgeting should be lean and agile, with a focus on cost-effective strategies that build awareness and drive initial customer acquisition. Bootstrapping[13] works great at this stage and is often necessary.

---

13 Bootstrapping is like being the MacGyver of business finance. It's all about starting and growing your business using nothing but your own savings, sheer grit, and the cash flow from initial sales. Imagine launching a rocket with nothing but a slingshot and some serious

- **For Growing Businesses:** Allocate funds towards scaling successful marketing tactics and exploring new channels for expansion.
- **For Established Companies:** Focus on optimizing existing channels, customer retention, and maximizing lifetime customer value.

---

elbow grease. That's bootstrapping. You're not relying on outside investors or hefty loans; instead, you're tightening your belt, getting creative with resources, and fueling your business dream with your own hard-earned cash.

Marketing Mirror

Reflect on your current marketing budget allocation. Are there areas where you might be overspending or underspending?

_____

_____

How do you decide which marketing channels to invest in?

_____

_____

Case Study: A Tale of Tactical Budgeting

Let's consider the story of a company we will call 'EcoEssentials', a small but growing company specializing in eco-friendly household products. Initially, EcoEssentials tried to compete with big brands in expensive ad spaces and quickly realized it was unsustainable. They came to me for assistance with a budgeting strategy that matched their size and growth stage.

By applying the principles of prudent budgeting, EcoEssentials shifted their focus to content marketing and community building on social media. They started a blog with tips on living sustainably, which was shared widely and brought significant traffic to their site. They also leveraged user-generated content to increase engagement and trust without incurring inflated costs.

While ads always cost money, these strategies can as well if you're hiring help, so don't assume that it was all free. This case study isn't about lowering their budget but using it in a way that's more efficient.

This strategic reallocation of resources allowed EcoEssentials to grow their customer base and increase brand loyalty without breaking the bank. Their story exemplifies how a business can implement a budgeting strategy that supports growth without stifling potential.

Resource Reallocation for Real Results

The ability to adapt is not just an advantage—it's a necessity. This is especially true when it comes to budgeting for marketing, where the landscape is constantly shifting under the influence of new technologies, consumer behaviors, and market trends. The art of reallocation is about staying responsive to these changes and ensuring that every dollar you spend is working as hard as it can for your business.

The Art of Reallocation

Periodic review and adjustment of your budget allocations are crucial. It's like pruning a garden; by cutting back the underperforming areas, you can redirect nutrients to the ones poised to bloom. Here's how to approach this:

- **Regular Reviews:** Set a regular schedule to review your marketing budget. This could be monthly, quarterly, or bi-annually, depending on the size and pace of your business. Put it on your calendar, even if that means it's just a meeting with yourself.
- **Performance Metrics:** Use clear performance metrics– and the correct ones–to assess the success of each marketing channel and strategy. If certain initiatives are not meeting expectations, it may be time to reallocate those funds.
- **Market Trends:** Stay informed about the latest marketing trends. If there's a shift towards a new channel or strategy that aligns with your business goals, consider reallocating resources to experiment with these new opportunities.
- **Feedback Loops:** Create feedback loops with your sales team, customer service, and even directly with customers to get a sense of what's working and what's not. Use this feedback to inform your re-allocation decisions.

Maximizing ROI

The ultimate goal of reallocation is to maximize your ROI. This means being ruthless with underperforming strategies and doubling down on the ones that yield results. Consider the following:

- **Cut the Slack:** If a particular marketing effort is not delivering, and you've given it time to stick (that's important), don't be afraid to cut it from your budget. It's better to invest in areas that show tangible returns.
- **Invest in Winners:** When you find a winning strategy, be prepared to invest more. Increasing your spend on high-performing channels can exponentially increase your returns. Just be sure that it doesn't end up as the *only* channel.
- **Balance Experimentation and Stability:** While it's important to invest in proven strategies, also set aside a portion of your budget for experimentation to discover potential new revenue streams.

Case Study: A Strategic Shift to Success

Consider the company that we will refer to as TechTrendz, a mid-sized company specializing in consumer electronics. They had a significant portion of their marketing budget tied up in traditional advertising channels, where it had always been, but the ROI was steadily declining over several years. They came to me for recommendations, and after a thorough review, we noticed that their content marketing efforts, particularly their instructional video series on

YouTube, were yielding a much higher engagement and conversion rate.

TechTrendz made the strategic decision to reallocate funds from traditional advertising to digital content creation. They invested in better production equipment, hired a small team dedicated to video content, and doubled down on their SEO efforts to increase the visibility of their videos.

The results were striking. Within six months, their online sales had increased by 35%, and their customer engagement metrics had improved across the board. TechTrendz's experience is a testament to the power of resource reallocation. By shifting their budget to where the results were, they were able to achieve real, measurable business growth.

The Investment Perspective

When you're pouring funds into your marketing efforts, it's crucial to see every penny as a seed planted for your business's future growth, not merely as an expense to be minimized. This shift in perspective is fundamental for long-term success and sustainability.

Every Penny Counts

When budgeting your marketing, a strategic investment mindset is key. It's not about how much you spend, but how you spend it. Your marketing budget isn't a black hole; it's fertile ground where strategic investments can yield substantial returns.

Invest Before it's Critical

Where I see so many entrepreneurs go wrong is when they are at that tipping point that so many businesses reach during their growth towards million-dollar years; you're in the mindset of still trying to do all of your marketing for free, yet you also know that it's time that you must invest to grow.

Not making investment in expert marketing soon enough can be the difference between growing and closing.

I've seen this with several clients in the past, who tried far too long to do everything on their own; and when they finally decided to get help, they were in a spot where they really didn't have enough runway left in their budget to do the marketing they actually needed. Waiting too long to invest in marketing can be like trying to climb out of a deep hole with a broken ladder – the longer you wait, the deeper the hole gets, and the harder it becomes to find a way out.

In these situations, the necessary investment to turn things around often exceeds what's available, leaving businesses in a precarious position where even the most effective marketing strategies might not be enough to salvage the situation.

If you find yourself calculating, "**If we don't close X deals, we'll have to shut down in Y months**," then it's a clear signal that professional assistance is not just needed but overdue. While there are still strategies and options to explore at this stage, the reality is that **seeking expert guidance earlier rather than later** opens up a broader range of possibilities and could be the difference between turning things around and facing closure.

Long-term Thinking

Strategic budgeting and resource allocation are the cornerstones of enduring business prosperity. They require a balance between immediate needs and future goals. This isn't just about the immediate impact on your bottom line; it's about setting the stage for ongoing success and reaching those pivotal milestones in your business journey.

Pivoting with Purpose

As you navigate the financial aspects of your marketing strategy, remember the power of the pivot. When a particular tactic isn't yielding the expected results (after you've given it enough time to stick), don't hesitate to redirect your funds to more fruitful endeavors. This isn't a misstep; it's a strategic move towards better outcomes. It's about being agile and responsive to the ever-evolving market landscape, ensuring that your marketing investments continue to support your business's growth trajectory.

Tools for Budgeting Success

When it comes to managing your marketing budget, the right tools and techniques can make all the difference. It's not just about how much you spend, but how wisely you allocate your funds.

Let's explore some strategies that can help you manage your marketing budget more effectively.

Budgeting Tools and Techniques

First, consider the tools at your disposal. There are various budgeting tools and software that can help you track your spending, forecast future costs, and analyze the effectiveness of your marketing efforts. Tools like spreadsheets can be a good start for those new to budgeting, but as your business grows, you might want to consider more sophisticated software that can offer deeper insights.

One approach is to redirect unfocused marketing dollars towards strategies with a proven ROI. For example, if you're spending money on graphic design software but it's not directly contributing to sales, it might be time to reallocate those funds to more impactful areas like lead generation or pay-per-click advertising.

From Planning to Execution

Putting your marketing budget plan into action requires a step-by-step approach:

- **Set Clear Goals:** Define what you want to achieve with your marketing efforts. This could be increasing brand awareness, driving sales, or growing your email list.
- **Allocate Funds Strategically:** Distribute your budget based on the goals you've set. Prioritize strategies that align with your objectives and have the potential for the best return on investment.
- **Monitor and Adjust:** Keep a close eye on your spending and the results it's yielding. Be prepared to adjust your budget allocation as you learn what works best for your business.
- **Measure Results:** Use analytics to measure the effectiveness of your marketing strategies. Look at metrics like conversion rates, cost per acquisition, and return on ad spend to evaluate success.
- **Refine Your Approach:** Based on your measurements, refine your marketing strategies. If something isn't working, don't be afraid to cut it from your budget and try something new.

The Magic of Mindful Spending

In conclusion, managing a marketing budget effectively is a balance of art and science. It requires a strategic approach, the right tools, and a willingness to adapt based on performance data.

Remember, every penny of your marketing budget should be considered an investment. By focusing on strategies that offer measurable returns, you can ensure that your marketing efforts contribute to your business's growth in a meaningful way.

Next Steps

Take a proactive approach to your marketing budget. Use the insights and strategies discussed to make informed financial decisions. Start by evaluating your current spending and look for opportunities to improve. Consider investing in budgeting tools that can provide deeper insights and help streamline the process. And always keep your business goals at the forefront of your budgeting decisions.

By being mindful of where and how you spend your marketing dollars, you can maximize the impact of every dollar spent and drive your business towards greater success.

Key Takeaways

- Balance your budget, time, and strategies to maximize the impact of your marketing efforts.

- Allocate resources based on strategic priorities and potential ROI.

- Understand the interplay between different marketing channels and allocate accordingly.

- Continuously evaluate and adjust your allocation strategy to optimize marketing performance.

The Data Detour

Introduction to Data Tracking

It's all too easy to fall into the data tracking trap. You're told to monitor everything—every click, every view, every fleeting interaction (and, as I already mentioned, every wrong metric).

But here's the thing: not all data is created equal. As you stand at the crossroads of data collection, it's crucial to discern which paths will lead you to valuable insights and which will send you spiraling into the abyss of analysis paralysis.

The Data Tracking Trap

The trap is set with good intentions: track everything to understand everything. Yet, this approach can quickly become a quagmire. When you're knee-deep in data points that don't align with your business objectives, you're not just wasting time—you're missing out on the data that truly matters.

It's like trying to find a needle in a haystack, except you keep adding more and more hay.

Quality Over Quantity

The key is to **prioritize quality over quantity**. It's not about how much data you have; it's about having *the right*

169

data. The data that cuts through the noise and gives you a clear signal. The data that informs decision-making should be your North Star, guiding your strategy and illuminating the path to your business goals. It's about collecting with **intention**, analyzing with **purpose**, and acting on data that drives **decisions**.

The Data Dead-Ends

Navigating the complex world of data tracking in marketing is akin to finding your way through a dense forest. It's not the quantity of data you collect that matters, but the quality and relevance to your strategic goals. Identifying and eliminating redundant metrics is crucial to maintaining a clear path to actionable insights.

Identifying Redundant Metrics

To avoid the clutter of unnecessary data, it's essential to discern which metrics serve your strategic goals and which are mere distractions. For example, high page views or a large number of social media followers might seem promising, but they don't necessarily equate to business growth or customer engagement.

Instead, prioritize metrics that offer real insights into customer behavior and campaign performance, such as:

- **Conversion Rates:** These are the compass that points to the effectiveness of your marketing efforts. By focusing on the steps that lead a visitor to become a customer, you can fine-tune your strategies to enhance the customer journey.

- **Customer Demographics:** Understanding who your customers are allows you to tailor your marketing efforts more effectively, ensuring that your message reaches the right audience.
- **Engagement Metrics:** Engagement goes beyond surface-level interactions. It's about measuring the depth of your audience's interaction with your content and how it influences their decision-making process.

Marketing Mirror

Can you recall a time when too much data led to a confusing or suboptimal marketing decision?

_____

_____

How do you currently filter and prioritize the data you collect for marketing decisions?

_____

_____

Case Study: Streamlining for Strategic Focus

Take the example of my client that was a boutique retail store and came to me tracking a ton of metrics, from website hits to the size of their email list. This approach led to an overwhelming amount of data but little understanding of what drove sales. (It also took a LOT of their time.)

Together we identified the most important indicators that would help them understand when things were going in the right direction, and when they were not. By shifting their focus to KPIs that mattered—like the **conversion rates** of their email campaigns and the **engagement levels** on new product launches—they were able to cut through the noise. This strategic move not only saved time but also uncovered the most effective tactics for their business growth.

The lesson here is clear: by eliminating redundant metrics, the boutique could concentrate on the data that truly informed their marketing decisions. This led to a more streamlined approach, enabling them to allocate their resources more efficiently and to replicate strategies that had a tangible impact on their bottom line.

In essence, the journey through the data doesn't require a trail of breadcrumbs in the form of excessive metrics. By focusing on the right indicators, you can forge a path to strategic clarity and marketing success.

Metrics that Matter

The true north of your compass should always point towards **Key Performance Indicators (KPIs)** that align with your business objectives. These indicators are not just numbers on a chart; they are beacons that guide your business decisions and strategies.

It's important to remember that the KPIs that you use to track should be as unique as your business and goals.

173

Key Performance Indicators (KPIs)

KPIs are the vital signs of your business's health. They are carefully selected metrics that give you the most accurate reading of your company's performance in relation to your strategic goals.

The art of selecting the right KPIs lies in understanding what you want to achieve. Is it more website conversions, increased customer retention, or higher sales? Once your goals are clear, you can identify which KPIs will serve as reliable markers of progress towards those goals.

For instance, if your goal is to enhance customer engagement on your website, your KPIs might include:

- **Average Time on Page:** Indicates the relevance and quality of your content.
- **Repeat Customer Rate:** Reflects customer satisfaction and loyalty.
- **Net Promoter Score (NPS):** Measures the likelihood of customers recommending your business.

Actionable Insights

The next step is to interpret the data from these KPIs to extract actionable insights. This means looking beyond the numbers to understand the story they tell about customer behavior, campaign effectiveness, and market trends. For example, a low average time on page might suggest that your content is not engaging or relevant to your audience, prompting a review and revision of your content strategy.

174

Case Study: Focusing on the Right Metrics

Consider the story of an entrepreneur who ran a local coffee shop Cobblestone Brew Café. She initially focused on the number of new customers as their primary metric. They scheduled a package of Fractional CMO sessions with me to discuss their overall strategy.

They soon realized that while new customers were important, the real growth driver was repeat business plus upsells. By shifting their focus to KPIs related to customer retention, such as repeat customer rate and purchase frequency, they were able to tailor their marketing efforts to encourage repeat visits.

The shop implemented loyalty programs, personalized marketing campaigns, and focused on providing exceptional customer service to make those customers want to return. As a result, they not only saw an increase in repeat customers but also an uptick in word-of-mouth referrals, leading to a significant impact on their bottom line.

By concentrating on the metrics that truly mattered, the entrepreneur turned data into a powerful tool for business growth. This approach underscores the importance of selecting and focusing on the right KPIs to drive informed decisions and strategic actions that align with your business objectives.

The Detour to Relevance

Data is your roadmap in your marketing journey, but it's crucial to navigate this roadmap wisely to reach the destination of business growth, since the path from raw data to a refined marketing strategy is paved with the insights you gather and the actions you take based on those insights.

Just like you've heard the adage about climbing the ladder, only to find it was against the wrong wall, following the wrong data can take you to the wrong destination.

From Data to Strategy

To effectively transform data into strategy, you need to adopt a two-pronged approach: interpret the data accurately and then apply those interpretations to refine your marketing tactics. Here's how you can do it:

- **Set Clear Objectives:** Before diving into data, know what you're looking for. What are your marketing objectives, what are your overall business goals, and what data do you need to measure progress towards these goals? KPIs should all feed into your overarching goals - one of which, of course, should be profit (not just revenue).
- **Segment Your Data:** Break down your data into segments that reflect different customer behaviors, campaign performances, or product sales. This will help you identify patterns and trends that are relevant to your objectives.

- **Test and Learn:** Use A/B testing to see how changes in your marketing strategy affect your KPIs. This can help you understand what works best for your audience.
- **Iterate Quickly:** Don't wait for perfect data. Use what information you have to make informed decisions, then refine your approach as more data comes in.
- **Focus on Actionable Data:** Always ask, "What can I do with this information?" If data doesn't lead to action, it may not be worth your focus.

Avoiding Analysis Paralysis

Analysis paralysis occurs when you become so overwhelmed by data that decision-making comes to a standstill. To avoid this, implement the following strategies:

- **Limit Your Focus:** Concentrate on a few key metrics that directly relate to your business goals. Too many metrics can dilute your focus and impede decision-making. Your primary metric should be profit, but many things will feed into that.
- **Set Data Review Cycles:** Schedule regular intervals to review your data. This prevents the constant checking of metrics, which can lead to over-analysis.
- **Embrace Imperfection:** Accept that not all data will be perfect or complete. Make the best decisions you can with the information at hand and be prepared to adjust as you go.
- **Use Dashboards:** Utilize data dashboards that aggregate your KPIs in one place. Developing a custom dashboard, where you can see all of those primary KPIs

in one place, can save a lot of precious time, since you aren't having to review multiple reports. I love using automations through Google Looker Studio for this setup.

- **Decide with Data, Act with Agility:** Use data to guide your decisions but remain agile. The digital landscape changes rapidly, and your ability to adapt is a competitive advantage.

By following these steps, you can ensure that your journey through the terrain of data leads you to the oasis of relevance—where every piece of information has a clear purpose in shaping your marketing strategies. This approach will keep you on the path to growth, avoiding the detours that lead to data overload and indecision.

Pivot: Simplifying Your Data Strategy

As we've already shown, data is abundant, but the key to a successful marketing strategy is not to capture more data, but to capture better data. Simplifying your data strategy can lead to clearer insights and more effective actions.

Tools for Efficient Tracking

There are numerous tools and software options available that can streamline the process of tracking the right data. These tools can automate data collection and provide you with real-time insights:

- **Analytics Platforms:** Utilize platforms like Google Analytics for comprehensive data on website traffic and user behavior.
- **CRM Systems:** Customer Relationship Management (CRM) systems can help track customer interactions and sales data.
- **Social Media Tools:** Tools like Hootsuite or Buffer offer analytics for social media engagement and performance, as do the platforms themselves.
- **Email Marketing Software:** Platforms such as Mailchimp provide detailed reports on email campaign performance.
- **Dashboard**: I like to pull as many metrics as possible into one dashboard using Google Looker Studio, with an overall snapshot dashboard on the front page, and other platform- specific reports on their own page feeding into the front page.

By integrating these tools into your marketing stack, you can efficiently track the metrics that are most relevant to your business goals.

The Lean Data Approach

The lean data approach is about stripping away the non-essentials and focusing on data that drives decision-making. Here's how to adopt this approach:

- **Prioritize:** Identify the top three to five metrics that matter most to your business objectives and concentrate on those.

- **Automate:** Set up automated reports for your key metrics so you can spend less time gathering data and more time using it.
- **Review Regularly:** Establish a routine to review your data, allowing you to make adjustments to your strategy as needed. Quick, consistent reviews are easier than once-a-year deep dives.
- **Simplify Reporting:** Create simple, visual reports that communicate your data clearly to stakeholders.

The Road Ahead with Data

As we conclude this section, remember that the goal of data tracking is not to collect as much information as possible, but to collect the right information that will inform your marketing decisions.

Next Steps

Take a moment to audit your current data tracking practices. Are you focusing on the metrics that truly matter? Are you using tools efficiently? If not, consider implementing a lean data strategy. By doing so, you can ensure that every piece of data you collect has a purpose and contributes to the overall success of your marketing efforts.

In the end, the data chosen should lead to actionable insights, strategic decisions, and, ultimately, business growth. Embrace the lean data approach and let the data help choose the path to your marketing goals.

Key Takeaways

- Use data intelligently and strategically to enhance your marketing decisions.

- Develop a structured approach to data analysis to avoid information overload.

- Leverage data to uncover insights into customer behavior and market trends.

- Use data-driven insights to refine your marketing strategies and achieve better results.

Part III: Laying the Groundwork for Growth

In the third leg of our journey (and don't worry we will stop for snacks soon), we turn our gaze inward, to the core of your enterprise. This is where we lay the groundwork for growth, not through a one-size-fits-all blueprint, but by understanding the unique blueprint of your business DNA. It's about recognizing that your business is as unique as you are and that its marketing must be equally bespoke.

Understanding Your Unique Business DNA is more than a chapter; it's a revelation. It's the moment you realize that your business isn't just another entity in the marketplace— it's a living, breathing organism with its own distinct characteristics. This section is about peeling back the layers to discover what makes your business tick, what sets it apart, and how to leverage that uniqueness in a crowded marketplace.

Building a Scalable Marketing Foundation is not just about laying bricks; it's about choosing the right materials that will support your business as it expands. We'll discuss the principles of creating marketing strategies that grow with you, that are flexible and robust enough to adapt to the changing tides of the market.

The Integration Imperative is where we see the individual components of your marketing strategy come together in a symphony of synchronized efforts. It's about creating a cohesive narrative across all platforms and touchpoints. Through the success story of a business that mastered this integration, we'll see the transformative power of a unified marketing approach.

In Part III, you'll discover the bedrock upon which you can build a towering edifice of business success.

What's in it for you? A profound understanding of your business's unique identity, a blueprint for scalable growth, and an integrated marketing strategy that resonates with the very core of your entrepreneurial spirit.

Let's embark on this introspective journey and lay the foundations that will stand the test of time.

Understanding Your Unique Business DNA

Introduction to Business Uniqueness

Every business carries a unique genetic code—a set of defining characteristics that dictate its strengths, weaknesses, opportunities, and threats. This is the business's unique DNA, an intrinsic blueprint that shapes its identity and potential for growth. Recognizing and understanding this DNA is not just beneficial; it's a critical component of any successful marketing strategy.

The notion that a single marketing strategy could fit every business is as outdated as it is ineffective and one of the most common mistakes that I see entrepreneurs make. The digital age demands a more bespoke approach, one that is as unique as the fingerprint of the business it aims to promote.

Bespoke Strategies for Bespoke Audiences

Your business's DNA is the key to unlocking a connection with your audience. It's about more than just the products or services you offer; it's the story behind your brand, the values you stand for, and the unique solutions you provide to your customers' problems.

By weaving these elements into your marketing narrative, you create a tailored message that resonates deeply with your target audience.

Competitive Edge in a Saturated Market

Nowadays consumers are constantly bombarded with countless choices, so your business's unique DNA can be the deciding factor that sets you apart. It's the secret sauce that differentiates your offerings from the competition.

When your marketing strategies are aligned with what makes your business unique, you're not just another option; you become the preferred choice.

Sustainable Growth Through Authenticity

Authenticity is the currency of the modern marketplace. Consumers are drawn to businesses that stay true to their roots and communicate their uniqueness transparently.

By understanding and embracing your business's DNA, your marketing efforts become more than just campaigns; they become the authentic expression of your brand's identity, fostering trust and loyalty among your customers.

The Myth of the Niche

The advice to "find your niche" is dispensed as frequently as business cards at a networking event. But is this always the golden ticket to success it's touted to be? No...because so many of the Fakexperts are **getting it wrong**.

Let's explore the nuances of this concept and explore why the niche narrative may not be the one-size-fits-all solution.

Beyond the Niche Narrative

The term 'niche' has been bandied about with such frequency in the marketing world that it's often taken as gospel.

However, the **original concept of a niche** in marketing is not about restricting yourself to a narrow audience but *finding a corner of the market where your unique value shines brightest.*

It's actually about your product or service, *not your audience*. It's about differentiation, not limitation.

The Misconception of Niching Down

Many entrepreneurs believe that niching down means they must turn away opportunities that don't fit into a narrowly defined category. This misconception can lead to missed opportunities and a business model that's too rigid to adapt to market changes.

Instead, understanding your niche should be about recognizing where **your strengths** intersect with a market need, without excluding potential growth avenues.

The Dual-Audience Approach

It's perfectly viable to have a primary target market while also catering to secondary audiences. This approach can safeguard against market fluctuations and inspire innovation by applying your expertise in different contexts.

For instance, a social media company might specialize in serving a particular industry due to the founder's background while also embracing local businesses that could benefit from their services - a niche self-imposed limitation I helped a peer overcome.

Case Study: The Balancing Act

Consider the case of a local event photography company with a strong foothold in a specific industry thanks to the founder's extensive experience. While most of their clientele comes from this sector, the desire to serve a broader audience persists.

She has had a couple of prospects from a larger segment approach her, and it's companies that she would LOVE to work with, but since *everyone* keeps telling her to "focus on your niche" she's wondering if she should turn the work away.

I reminded her that the solution isn't to niche down further, but to **embrace a dual-audience strategy**. By doing so, the company can maintain its authority in its primary market while also expanding its reach to local businesses, enjoying the best of both worlds.

The Power of Flexibility

In the pursuit of a niche, **rigidity can be the enemy**. The key is to remain flexible and responsive to the market's needs. For example, a business might start by serving a broad audience and, through consistent engagement and data analysis, discover a specific offering that resonates strongly with a segment of their audience. This insight allows them to refine their focus without being constrained by some arbitrary niche from the outset.

The question of whether to niche or not is not a binary one. It's about balance, flexibility, and the strategic use of data to inform your decisions. By understanding the true meaning of a niche and the importance of a dual-audience approach, businesses can craft a marketing strategy that is both focused and adaptable, ensuring long-term growth and resilience in the marketplace.

Discovering Your Uniqueness

Your business's uniqueness is not just a trait—it's your **secret weapon**. It's what sets you apart in a sea of competitors and beckons your ideal customers to your door.

But how do you unearth these distinguishing features? It's a journey of introspection and analysis, a process that requires you to dig deep into the ethos of your brand and the essence of your offerings.

Remember my client Cobblestone Brew Café? They're a small artisan coffee shop that sources beans from sustainable farms and offers a cozy reading nook. This isn't just a place to get your caffeine fix—it's an experience, a community hub, a statement of values. And I will admit that the reading nook is the favorite spot for a book nerd like me!

Or consider the tech startup whose software isn't just innovative, but also prioritizes user privacy in a way that others don't. These businesses have identified what makes them unique and have woven it into the very fabric of their brand.

Marketing Mirror

What are the unique aspects of your business, and how do they influence your marketing strategies?

_____

_____

Can you identify a time when your marketing strategy failed to reflect your unique business DNA?

_____

_____

Defining Your Unique Selling Points (USPs)

Understanding and defining your Unique Selling Points (USPs) - sometimes also called Unique Value Propositions (UVPs) - is like uncovering the hidden gems that make your business sparkle in the sunlight of the marketplace. (Note that I prefer the term USPs because I feel like keeping the focus on the word "selling" is important for any entrepreneur.)

It's about pinpointing those key aspects that make your offerings irresistible to your target audience. A USP could be anything from a product feature that no one else offers, to an exceptional level of service, or a company ethos that resonates deeply with your customers.

One of the biggest mistakes I see many entrepreneurs make is to say low price is one of their USPs or differentiators. It should *never be* price. Too many fluctuations in the market can impact that, and if suddenly you need to raise your price, then you have nothing different.

To define your USPs, start by looking at what you provide that your competitors don't.

- ☐ Is there a problem that only your product solves?
- ☐ Do you deliver your services faster, or with a personal touch that others lack?
- ☐ Are your business practices being more sustainable?
- ☐ Are your products handcrafted with a level of quality that is unmatched?

These types of differentiators are the factors that will not only attract customers but also retain them.

When considering your USPs, it's also essential to think about the scalability and sustainability of these unique factors. As your business grows, can these selling points grow with it? Will they continue to set you apart even as the market evolves? It's not enough to be unique for the moment; your USPs should be the cornerstones of your long-term strategy.

Interactive: Unveiling Your Business Uniqueness

To help you in this journey of discovery, this step-by-step guide will assist you in drilling down to the core of what makes your business special. It's a process that asks probing questions about your values, your mission, and the impact you want to have on your customers and the world.

The worksheet will lead you through a series of exercises designed to help you look beyond the surface-level features of your products or services. You'll explore the emotional and psychological aspects of your brand—how does it make people feel, what does it stand for, and why does it matter? By the end of this process, you'll have a set of clearly defined USPs that you can communicate with confidence.

This self-discovery isn't just a marketing exercise; it's a strategic foundation. Knowing your USPs informs everything from product development to customer service, to your brand story. It's about aligning every facet of your business with the unique value you offer, ensuring that every touchpoint with customers reinforces why they chose you in the first place.

Your USPs are the lighthouses that guide customers to your shores. They are the declarations of what you stand for and the promises of what you deliver. By clearly defining and consistently delivering on your USPs, you create a business that stands out, attracts, and retains a loyal customer base.

Section 1: Core Values and Mission

Identify Your Core Values: List the top five values that are at the heart of your business. How do these values influence your daily operations and decision-making?

1.
2.
3.
4.
5.

Define Your Mission: What is your business's primary goal beyond making a profit? How does this mission guide your strategies and interactions with customers?

Section 2: Emotional and Psychological Impact

Emotional Connection: Describe the emotions you want your brand to evoke in your customers. Is it trust, excitement, comfort, or something else?

Brand Personality: If your brand were a person, how would you describe its personality? Is it friendly, authoritative, innovative, traditional, etc.?

Section 3: Unique Selling Propositions (USPs)

Identifying USPs: What makes your products or services unique compared to your competitors? Consider aspects like quality, price, customer service, technology, etc.

Articulating USPs: How do you communicate these unique aspects to your customers? Are they clearly reflected in your marketing materials, website, and customer interactions?

Section 4: Customer Impact and Brand Storytelling

Customer Transformation: How does your product or service transform your customers' lives? Think about the before and after scenario for your customers.

Brand Storytelling: What story does your brand tell? How does this story resonate with your target audience and differentiate you in the market?

_____

_____

Section 5: Strategic Alignment

Aligning Operations with USPs: How are your USPs reflected in your business operations, from product development to customer service?

_____

_____

Consistency Check: Evaluate your current marketing efforts. Are they consistently aligned with your USPs?

_____

_____

Section 6: Future Vision and Goals

Long-term Vision: Where do you see your business in the next 5 years? How do your USPs fit into this vision?

_____

_____

Setting Goals: Based on your USPs, what are your immediate and long-term goals for your business?

_____

_____

This worksheet is designed to be a starting point in your journey to uncover the unique aspects of your business. It's

196

thorough enough to provide valuable insights, but remember, the path to fully realizing and leveraging your USPs often requires professional guidance. Don't hesitate to reach out for expert help to refine and implement these discoveries into your business strategy.

Tailoring Strategies to Your Business DNA

Crafting marketing strategies that are a perfect fit for your business's unique DNA is akin to tailoring a bespoke suit—it should accentuate the strengths, fit perfectly, and adapt to changes over time. It's about creating a strategy that is as unique as your business's fingerprint, one that resonates with your core values and speaks directly to your target audience.

To begin, take a deep look into what makes your business tick.

- What are your core values?
- Who is your ideal customer?
- What is the mission that drives your operations?

The answers to these questions should be the guiding stars of your marketing strategy. They should influence every decision; from the platforms you choose to the messaging you craft.

However, it's crucial to be aware of common pitfalls in this process.

197

One such pitfall is the **echo chamber effect**, where you create a strategy so unique that it only resonates with a super-niche audience that's too small to sustain business growth.

Another is the temptation to *be different for the sake of difference* instead of authentic differentiation, which can lead to gimmicky tactics that don't genuinely connect with your audience.

To avoid these traps, ensure your strategies are **grounded in market research** and customer feedback. Your unique business DNA should inform your strategy, but not at the expense of relevance and resonance with your audience. It's a delicate balance between being true to your business and adaptable to the market.

Effective strategies also consider the competitive landscape.

- What are your competitors doing, and how can you do it better or differently?

Your USPs should be the spearhead of your strategy, differentiating you from the competition and highlighting the unique benefits you offer.

A marketing strategy tailored to your business DNA is not a static document; it's a living, breathing blueprint that **evolves** as your business and the market change. It requires constant refinement and a willingness to pivot when necessary.

By staying true to your unique characteristics and remaining flexible, you can create a marketing strategy that not only stands out but also delivers tangible results.

Case Studies: Success Beyond the Niche

When it comes to transcending the confines of a niche, there are businesses that have turned their unique DNA into their superpower. Let's explore a few case studies that exemplify success beyond the niche.

Case Study 1: The Artisanal Bakery That Became a Community Hub

Consider the story of a small artisanal bakery we will call Whisk & Crumb Boulangerie that decided to focus on its passion for community and sustainability rather than just selling baked goods. They used locally sourced ingredients and transformed the bakery into a community hub where people could learn about sustainable practices.

Their marketing strategy revolved around their story and values, which resonated deeply with customers.

They didn't just sell bread; they sold an experience and a vision for a better world.

Case Study 2: The Tech Startup That Prioritized User Privacy

In the crowded tech space, the startup FortiGuardian decided to make user privacy its core tenet. In an era where data breaches are common, they communicated their commitment to privacy through every marketing channel. They offered transparent policies and robust security features that set them apart from giants in the industry.

Their dedication to privacy won them a loyal customer base that valued their unique stance in a market often criticized for its lack of privacy.

Case Study 3: The Fashion Brand That Celebrated All Body Types

The fashion brand AlluraMosaic Fashion decided to challenge the industry norms by celebrating inclusivity and body positivity. They showcased models of all sizes, ages, and backgrounds, making a strong statement against the one-size-fits-all approach.

Their marketing campaigns highlighted their commitment to diversity, which not only set them apart but also sparked a movement within the fashion industry.

Embracing Your Business Identity

The journey of discovering and embracing your business's unique DNA is transformative. It's about peeling back the layers to reveal the core of what makes your business truly special. This process is not about fitting into a predefined niche; it's about carving out your own space in the marketplace by being authentically you.

As we wrap up this section, remember that **your business identity is your strongest asset**. It's what sets you apart in a sea of competitors. By integrating this identity into your marketing efforts, you create a narrative that is not only authentic but also deeply engaging. Your unique business DNA should be the cornerstone of your marketing strategy, informing every decision and guiding every campaign.

Embrace the quirks, the ethos, and the values that define your business. Let them shine through in your marketing and watch as they resonate with your audience. This is not just about being different; it's about being true to what your business stands for. It's about building a brand that people can believe in and rally behind.

So, take this knowledge forward. Let it inform your marketing efforts and infuse your strategies with the kind of authenticity that can only come from a deep understanding of your unique business DNA. The market is ready for what you have to offer. It's time to show them what makes your business truly one-of-a-kind.

Key Takeaways

- Embrace what makes your business unique and align your marketing strategies accordingly.

- Conduct a thorough analysis of your business's strengths, weaknesses, opportunities, and threats.

- Tailor your marketing message to resonate with your unique audience and business values.

- Utilize your unique selling propositions (USPs) to differentiate your business in the market.

Building a Scalable Marketing Foundation

Introduction to Scalability in Marketing

Building a scalable marketing foundation is akin to constructing a sturdy, adaptable structure that can withstand the ebbs and flows of the business climate. Scalability in marketing refers to the ability to maintain or improve your profit margins while sales volume increases. This is achieved by creating systems and strategies that can grow with your business, without the need for a constant increase in resources.

The pursuit of scalability in marketing is *not* about jumping on every new trend that sweeps through the digital landscape. While staying current is important, the **misconception** that the latest social media craze or a fresh marketing gimmick is a golden ticket to growth can lead businesses astray. (No, you do not need to do TikTok dance videos, if that doesn't resonate with your brand message. Actually, even if it does, you still don't need to.) True scalability is about establishing a solid foundation of marketing practices that are effective, efficient, and most importantly, expandable.

This foundation is built on a deep understanding of your target audience, a clear articulation of your unique selling propositions (USPs), and a marketing strategy that leverages

203

both to reach your audience in the most impactful way. It's about setting up processes and utilizing tools that automate and streamline tasks, freeing up time and resources to focus on strategic decision-making and creative endeavors.

In the context of marketing, scalability means your strategies should be **designed to grow in tandem with your business**. It involves setting up a marketing infrastructure that supports expansion without the need for a proportional increase in marketing spend or effort.

This includes having a flexible content strategy that can be scaled up or down, using marketing automation tools to handle repetitive tasks, and employing tactics that have a compounding effect over time, such as SEO and content marketing.

By focusing on building a scalable marketing foundation, you're not just preparing for growth; you're ensuring that your marketing efforts contribute to sustainable business success. It's about making smart choices now that will pay dividends in the future, ensuring that your marketing engine not only supports growth but also drives it.

The Pitfalls of Trend-Chasing

It's easy to get caught up in the whirlwind of new trends and software that promise to revolutionize your business. However, the allure of these shiny new tools can sometimes lead to a treacherous path, one where the focus shifts from what's truly important—building a scalable and sustainable marketing foundation. SQUIRREL!

Chasing the latest marketing trends can be a slippery slope. It often starts with the best intentions; you want to keep your business ahead of the curve and tap into new strategies that could potentially unlock growth. Yet, this approach can quickly turn into a trap. The danger lies in becoming so enamored with new tools and tactics that you overlook the core of your marketing strategy—the systems and processes that are proven to work for your unique business.

The reality is that **new doesn't always mean better**. Really! Some of the strongest marketing strategies that I use with clients are those that have been around for decades!

For instance, the introduction of new marketing software might seem like the perfect solution to your current challenges. But without a clear understanding of your existing systems, this can lead to duplication of tasks, wasted resources, and a fragmented strategy. It's like trying to fit a big square peg into a small round hole; no matter how much you beat on it, it just won't fit.

Consider a scenario where a business coach recommends a **specific set of marketing tools** to achieve a particular goal. While their recommendation may come from a place of success in their own practice, it might not align with your business's needs or integrate well with your existing systems.

I see this often with some of the Fakexperts, who can only use the system that their marketing MLM person above them taught them. They don't have enough experience to integrate YOUR systems with any strategies they learned. This misalignment can result in increased costs, inefficiencies, and even confusion among your team as they juggle multiple overlapping tools.

Moreover, the commission-based recommendations from some coaches can further complicate the decision-making process. While there's nothing inherently wrong with earning commissions based upon platforms you recommend, such as part of affiliate marketing, it's crucial for you as the business owner to discern whether the recommended tools genuinely serve your business's best interests or if they're being suggested primarily for financial gain.

Focused Approach for Scalability

To build a scalable marketing foundation, it's essential to take a step back and evaluate the tools and strategies that will truly serve your long-term goals. This means resisting the temptation to jump on every new trend and instead, focusing on a marketing ecosystem that works cohesively to support your business's growth.

A focused approach to marketing scalability involves:

- **Understanding Your Current Systems:** Before adding new tools to your arsenal, take the time to fully comprehend the capabilities and limitations of your existing marketing technology. This will help you identify any gaps that need filling and avoid unnecessary duplication.

- **Aligning Tools with Goals:** Ensure that any new marketing software or strategy aligns with your business objectives. It should complement, not complicate, your current processes and contribute to a seamless customer journey.
- **Cost-Efficiency:** Evaluate the cost implications of new tools, not just in terms of subscription fees but also considering the time and resources required for implementation and maintenance.
- **Integration and Automation:** Opt for tools that integrate well with each other, allowing for automation that can save time and reduce the risk of errors.
- **Expert Consultation:** Seek advice from marketing experts who have a broad understanding of various tools and can provide unbiased recommendations based on your specific needs.

By adopting a focused and discerning approach to your marketing stack, you can avoid the pitfalls of trend-chasing and establish a scalable foundation that supports sustained growth. Remember, the goal is not to collect the most tools, but to curate a set of resources that work harmoniously to drive your business forward.

Core Principles of Scalable Marketing Strategies

Scalability is not just a buzzword; it's the backbone of a strategy that ensures your business can grow without being hampered by its own marketing efforts.

Scalability in marketing means creating a strategy that can expand in response to your business growth and market demands without requiring a complete overhaul or disproportionate increases in budget or resources.

Consistency: The Marketing Cornerstone

One of the foundational principles of scalable marketing strategies is consistency. This doesn't mean being monotonous or resistant to change. Rather, it's about maintaining a coherent brand image and message across all your marketing channels.

Just as you wouldn't appreciate your favorite bread being moved every time you visit the grocery store (I *hate* having to search for my regular purchases every time I visit … yet I completely understand from a marketing perspective why they do this), your customers appreciate familiarity in your marketing. A consistent marketing approach builds brand recognition and customer trust, making it easier for them to find and engage with your content.

Adaptability: The Agile Marketing Approach

While consistency is key, rigidity can be the downfall of many marketing strategies. Adaptability is the principle that allows your marketing to remain effective and relevant in the face of changing market conditions and consumer behaviors.

It's about being prepared to tweak and refine your strategies in response to feedback and data without losing sight of your core brand values and objectives.

Efficiency: Doing More with Less

Efficiency in marketing means maximizing the impact of your efforts while minimizing waste, whether it's time, money, or resources. It's about finding the most effective ways to reach and engage your audience without unnecessary complexity.

This could mean automating certain marketing tasks, using data to streamline your targeting, or simply ensuring that your marketing messages are clear and direct.

By focusing on these core principles, you can create marketing strategies that are not only scalable but also sustainable in the long term. Remember, the goal is to grow your business and its marketing efforts in tandem, ensuring that one supports the other without becoming a burden.

The 3x3 Marketing Matrix™

The 3x3 Marketing Matrix™ is a strategic framework I designed that helps entrepreneurs quickly categorize and

209

prioritize next step marketing tactics across three key areas: Communication, Funnel, and Value. It's laid out in a grid with three columns under these headings, and three rows labeled Current, Easy, and ROI.

Communication

This column focuses on how you interact with prospects and clients. It includes social media, email, and direct mail strategies.

Funnel

Here, we look at the journey your suspects and prospects take towards becoming customers. This involves your sales process and advertising efforts.

Value

The final column is about your product mix, how you differentiate from competitors, and understanding your client avatars.

How to Use the 3x3 Marketing Matrix

Current Strategies: Start by filling in the 'Current' row with the strategies you're currently employing in each of the three columns. This gives you a clear picture of your existing marketing efforts.

Easy Wins: In the 'Easy' row, identify new strategies that you can add that are low-hanging fruit—simple to implement and likely to yield quick results. These should be tactics that don't require a significant investment of time or resources but can enhance your current strategies.

High ROI Tactics: The 'ROI' row is for new tactics that, while they may require more effort or investment, promise a significant return. These are your long-term plays that will contribute to sustainable growth.

Adapting the Matrix to Your Business

The beauty of the 3x3 Marketing Matrix™ is its adaptability. It's not about the specific tactics you choose; it's about the strategic approach to selecting and implementing.

For example, a local bakery might use social media posts as a 'Current' strategy, add an 'Easy' strategy like a newsletter featuring special offers, and invest in a 'High ROI' strategy like a loyalty program that integrates with their POS.

Conversely, a tech startup might have current PPC campaigns, an 'Easy' strategy like optimizing their Google My Business listing, and a 'High ROI' strategy like developing a content marketing plan to establish thought leadership.

The 3x3 Marketing Matrix™ is a dynamic tool that helps you visualize and organize your marketing strategy for maximum efficiency and scalability. By focusing on current practices, easy wins, and high ROI tactics, you can create a balanced approach that grows with your business. Use this matrix as a living document, revisiting and revising it as your business and the market evolve.

Worksheet: 3x3™ Marketing Matrix

Here's a streamlined version of the Matrix for your use:

	Communicate	Funnel	Value
Current Strategy			
Easy Addition			
Biggest ROI			

Strategies for Scaling Your Marketing Efforts

Scaling your marketing efforts is akin to preparing a gourmet meal; you need the right ingredients, a solid recipe, and the ability to adjust to the taste preferences of your diners. (Yes, I like to cook. And I like to eat what is cooked lol.)

In recipe for business growth, exploring new markets and innovating are the spices that can transform a good dish into a great one. Let's unpack how to add these flavors to your marketing mix for a recipe that scales your business to new heights.

Exploring New Markets for Business Expansion

Venturing into new markets is like exploring uncharted culinary territories. It's an opportunity to discover new flavors and ingredients that can add depth to your business offerings. But it's not just about being adventurous; it's about strategic exploration aligned with your overall business goals, existing products, services, and audience.

Identifying Opportunities

New markets are the hidden gems in the business landscape. They offer fresh customer segments, diversify your product offerings, and enhance your brand's presence. By tapping into these markets, you can uncover hidden

213

potential and create new revenue streams that resonate with your business's core values and objectives.

Mitigating Risks

Diversification is your safety net in the high-wire act of business. By expanding into new markets, you reduce dependence on a single market, thereby minimizing the impact of local economic fluctuations or industry-specific downturns. This strategic move ensures stability and resilience, allowing your business to thrive even during uncertain times.

The Role of Innovation in Business Expansion

Innovation is the secret sauce of business growth. It's what differentiates a standard meal from a Michelin-star experience. In the context of scaling your marketing efforts, innovation is about finding new ways to engage with your audience, deliver your products, and communicate your brand's message.

Market Exploration

Market exploration is not just about geographic expansion; it's about finding new ways to serve existing markets or creating entirely new ones. It's about understanding the evolving tastes of your customers and adapting your offerings to meet those needs.

Innovation as a Growth Lever

Innovation should be at the heart of your scaling efforts. It's about leveraging new technologies, embracing new marketing platforms, and thinking outside the traditional advertising box. Whether it's through digital transformation or creative campaign strategies, innovation is what will keep your marketing efforts fresh and effective.

By incorporating insights and strategies while exploring new markets and the role of innovation in business expansion, you can craft a marketing plan that not only scales with your business but also ensures long-term success. The goal is to create a scalable marketing strategy that grows with your business, adapting to new challenges and seizing new opportunities as they arise.

Marketing Mirror

How does your current marketing strategy accommodate potential business growth?

What scalability challenges have you faced or anticipate in your marketing efforts?

Self-Assessment

Are you ready to grow? Answer each question with yes, no, or unsure. Remember, there are no right or wrong answers.

	Yes	No	Unsure
Does your existing marketing strategy easily adapt to changes in your business size, market trends, or customer behaviors?	☐	☐	☐
Are your resources (time, budget, manpower) capable of scaling up without compromising efficiency or effectiveness?	☐	☐	☐
Do you use tools and technology that can	☐	☐	☐

handle increased demand and complexity as your business grows?			
Is your marketing strategy flexible enough to accommodate new target markets or customer segments?	☐	☐	☐
Can your current methods of measuring marketing success scale with your business growth?	☐	☐	☐
Are you confident in maintaining brand consistency across all marketing channels, even as your campaigns expand?	☐	☐	☐

Have you encountered challenges in scaling your marketing efforts that make you consider seeking professional assistance?	☐	☐	☐

Scoring:

Mostly 'Yes': Your marketing strategy seems well-prepared for scaling. Keep monitoring and adjusting as your business grows.

Mostly 'No' or 'Unsure': It may be time to seek professional help to ensure your marketing strategy can effectively scale with your business.

Examples: Scaling Success Stories

Scaling a business's marketing efforts is a journey marked by strategic decisions and pivotal moments that can lead to exponential growth. Let's explore some real-life examples of well-known businesses that have successfully scaled their marketing strategies, pinpointing the tipping points that propelled their expansion and the savvy maneuvers they employed to sidestep common pitfalls.

- **Amazon**: From an online bookstore to a global e-commerce giant, Amazon's tipping point came with the introduction of Amazon Prime. This loyalty program not only increased customer retention but also diversified revenue streams. By consistently leveraging data analytics to understand customer behavior, Amazon avoided the pitfall of overexpansion without direction. And of course, a lesser-known pivot point was when they realized the cloud computing resources they were using was inhibiting their growth, so they built their own; and now Amazon Web Services (AWS) is actually their largest income generator.
- **Netflix**: Netflix transitioned from a DVD rental service to a streaming behemoth by capitalizing on the shift towards digital consumption. (A move that Blockbuster missed.) Their tipping point was the strategic decision to invest in original content, which differentiated them in a crowded market. They avoided the scaling pitfall of diluting brand value by ensuring their content was synonymous with quality and innovation.
- **Airbnb**: Starting as a simple platform to rent out spare rooms, Airbnb's expansion into a global community for unique accommodations was marked by a tipping point when they focused on user experience and trust. By implementing a robust review system and authentic photography, they sidestepped the pitfall of consumer skepticism that often hampers peer-to-peer platforms.

- **Tesla**: Tesla's surge from a niche electric car manufacturer to a leader in sustainable transportation can be traced back to the unveiling of the Model S. This tipping point showcased their commitment to innovation and design, attracting a broader market. They avoided the common pitfall of niche marketing by positioning their brand as aspirational and mainstream.
- **Apple**: Apple's ascent was catalyzed by the launch of the iPod, turning them from a computer company into a lifestyle brand. This pivotal product launch, coupled with the iTunes music store, revolutionized how people consumed media. Apple avoided the pitfall of product-centric marketing by creating an ecosystem that offered a seamless user experience.
- **Google**: Google's expansion beyond search into areas like mobile operating systems and cloud computing was marked by a focus on integration and user-centric design. The tipping point was the launch of Android, which opened up new markets and revenue channels. They avoided the pitfall of market saturation by offering an open-source platform that encouraged innovation and diversity.
- **Starbucks**: Starbucks transformed from a coffee retailer into a global icon by creating a 'third place' between work and home. The tipping point was the decision to focus on the customer experience rather than just the product. They avoided the pitfall of commoditization by emphasizing community and consistency across all locations.

Each of these brands showcases the importance of identifying and acting upon a strategic tipping point that aligns with the core business model and market trends. They demonstrate the necessity of avoiding common scaling pitfalls by maintaining a strong brand identity, focusing on customer experience, and leveraging innovation.

These stories serve as a blueprint for businesses aiming to scale their marketing efforts successfully. As the marketing landscape continues to shift, and more quickly than ever before, it will be interesting to see if they remain able to successfully pivot.

Building for the Future

In the pursuit of building a business that not only survives but **thrives**, establishing a scalable marketing foundation is not just a strategy—it's a necessity. The journey of the brands we've explored underscores the importance of foresight, adaptability, and a deep understanding of one's customers and market dynamics.

Building for the Future

- **Scalability is a Mindset:** Embrace the idea that your marketing efforts should grow with your business. This means being prepared to evolve and adapt your strategies as your business and the market change.
- **Customer-Centricity is Key:** Whether it's through loyalty programs, quality content, or a unique user

experience, successful scaling often hinges on how well you know and serve your customers.

- **Innovation as a Differentiator:** Standing out in a crowded market often requires bold moves and innovation. This could mean diversifying your offerings, like Amazon, or creating a new market, like Tesla.
- **Avoid Trend Traps:** Chasing the latest fads can lead to a dilution of your brand and a waste of resources. Focus on trends that align with your long-term vision and core competencies.
- **Data-Driven Decisions:** Use data analytics to guide your scaling efforts. This will help you make informed decisions and avoid the pitfalls of assumption-based expansion.
- **Integrated Experience:** Like Apple, create an ecosystem for your customers that provides a seamless and consistent experience across all touchpoints.
- **Quality Over Quantity:** It's not about being everywhere at once, but about being impactful where it matters most. Quality engagement with your audience will always trump sheer volume.
- **Community and Consistency:** Building a community around your brand, as Starbucks did, can foster loyalty and advocacy that fuels growth.

As you reflect on these insights, consider how they can be woven into the fabric of your own marketing plan. Scaling your marketing isn't about a one-off campaign or a sudden surge in budget—it's about building a resilient structure that supports sustainable growth over time.

Take these lessons and view them through the lens of your unique business.

- How can you apply these principles to your marketing efforts?
- What is your version of Amazon Prime or the iPod that will propel your business forward?

Identify your strengths, understand your customers, and build a marketing foundation that can support your business as it reaches new heights.

Remember, the future belongs to those who prepare for it today. By applying these scalable marketing principles, you're not just planning for the next quarter or the next year—you're building a legacy that can endure.

Key Takeaways

- Develop a robust and scalable marketing framework to accommodate growth and change.
- Focus on building a flexible marketing system that can adapt to business expansions or shifts.
- Implement scalable tools and processes that can grow with your business.
- Prepare for future growth by building a solid marketing foundation that supports scaling.

The Integration Imperative

The Essence of Integrated Marketing

Integrated marketing isn't just a buzzword; it's the backbone of any robust marketing strategy. You've likely heard the term, but what does it truly entail?

Integrated marketing is the harmonious symphony of your marketing efforts across various channels to create a unified, seamless brand experience for your customers. It's about ensuring that whether your audience encounters your brand on social media, in a newsletter, or through a Google search, they're met with a **consistent message** that resonates with your brand's core values.

Why is this so significant?

Because in the digital age, consumers are inundated with information from countless sources. Without integration, your message risks getting lost in the noise. Integrated marketing ensures that your brand's voice isn't just another echo, but a clear, consistent presence across the vast landscape of consumer touchpoints.

Breaking Down Silos

If you've ever felt that *your social media team is from Mars and your content creators are from Venus,* you're not alone. (And sometimes I think the bad advice out there is from

225

Uranus lol.) **Marketing silos** are much more common for a small business than we'd like to admit, and they're a surefire way to fragment your customer's experience.

When each team works in isolation, focused only on their channel's goals, the result is a disjointed narrative that confuses customers and dilutes your brand's message.

Breaking down these silos is crucial. It involves fostering communication and collaboration across all departments (or unifying the department into one). When the social media, content, SEO, and advertising teams and all others are aligned under a unified strategy, each channel reinforces the others, creating a marketing ecosystem that's more than the sum of its parts.

This unified approach doesn't just enhance the customer experience; it amplifies your brand's message, ensuring that no matter where your customers find you, they're met with the same story—one that's compelling, cohesive, and unmistakably yours.

Marketing Integration Checklist

- ☐ Consistent Branding Across Channels: Ensure your branding is consistent in tone, visuals, and messaging across all marketing channels.
- ☐ Aligned Marketing Objectives: Confirm that all marketing efforts align with your overarching business and marketing objectives.

- Cross-Channel Communication: Implement strategies for your marketing channels to support and enhance each other.
- Unified Customer Experience: Check that customer experiences are seamless and consistent across different platforms and touchpoints.
- Data and Insights Sharing: Ensure that insights and data are shared effectively between different marketing teams or tools.
- Coordinated Campaign Timing: Coordinate the timing of campaigns across various channels to maximize impact.
- Feedback Mechanisms: Have mechanisms in place to gather and act upon feedback from all marketing channels.
- Resource Allocation: Ensure resources are allocated efficiently across channels based on performance and objectives.

Case Study: A Tale of Transformation

Imagine a business we will call GadgetGo that started as a small online store for tech enthusiasts. GadgetGo had all the makings of a success story but was hampered by disjointed marketing efforts.

Their social media campaigns were clever and trendy, while their email marketing felt like a throwback to the early 1990s.

The website was optimized for search engines, but the content didn't align with the adverts running on other platforms (and it also looked like it was from 1990). It was a classic case of the right hand not knowing what the left was doing.

The Challenge

GadgetGo's main hurdle was **inconsistency**. Customers who clicked through from a sleek Instagram ad were jarred by the website's outdated design and mismatched messaging. The lack of cohesion led to customer confusion, a drop in trust, and, ultimately, lost sales.

The Integration Process

The transformation began with a comprehensive audit of all marketing channels to identify disconnects. Together with GadgetGo's leadership we brought together all of their various freelancers to create a unified vision. This is a common role I serve when acting as a Fractional CMO.

Together we all developed a brand bible that became the north star for all their marketing efforts, ensuring every piece of content, regardless of the channel, was on-brand and on-message.

We also recommended a marketing integration tool that allowed for seamless communication between different team members and platforms. This tool enabled them to track customer interactions across channels and ensure that the messaging was consistent at every touchpoint.

The Outcomes

Post-integration, GadgetGo saw a dramatic shift. Their customer engagement metrics soared as the unified brand experience began to resonate with their audience.

The consistent messaging across platforms led to a more robust brand identity and a significant increase in conversion rates. Perhaps most telling was the customer feedback; people loved the new cohesive experience, feeling a stronger connection to the GadgetGo brand.

This case study isn't just a success story; it's a roadmap. GadgetGo's journey from a fragmented to a harmonized marketing strategy underscores the power of integration. It's a testament to the fact that when a business aligns its efforts across all channels, the results can be transformative.

Strategies for Effective Integration

The key to effective integration lies in a symphony of strategies that ensure your message is harmonious across all channels.

Cross-Channel Alignment

Start by mapping out all your marketing channels and the journey your customer takes through each. Identify any discrepancies in messaging or branding and rectify them. Ensure that your brand's voice is unmistakable, whether a customer is reading an email, browsing your website, or scrolling through social media.

Cross-Functional Teams

Integration is a team sport. It requires breaking down the silos between departments (or freelancers) and fostering a culture of collaboration. Encourage regular cross-departmental meetings where teams can share insights and coordinate campaigns. This unity in communication is the bedrock upon which integrated marketing is built.

Consistent Customer Experience

Your customers don't see different departments; they see one brand. Ensure that the customer experience is consistent, whether they're dealing with sales, customer service, or marketing. This consistency builds trust and reinforces brand loyalty.

Technology and Integration

Technology is the glue that binds your integrated marketing strategies together. It's the enabler that turns your vision for a seamless customer experience into reality.

Marketing Automation Platforms

Invest in a robust marketing automation platform that can manage and synchronize campaigns across different channels. Look for features like customer segmentation, behavior tracking, and analytics to fine-tune your efforts.

CRM Systems

A Customer Relationship Management (CRM) system is crucial for maintaining a single source of truth about your customers. It can help personalize the customer experience by providing relevant information at every touchpoint.

Data Integration Tools

Use data integration tools to ensure that customer data flows freely and securely between systems. This real-time data exchange is vital for maintaining up-to-date customer profiles and delivering timely, relevant content.

Choosing the Right Tools

When selecting technological tools, consider not only their features but also their integration capabilities. They should easily connect with your existing systems to create a cohesive marketing ecosystem.

By leveraging these strategies and technologies, you can create a marketing orchestra that plays in perfect harmony, captivating your audience and leading them gracefully through the buyer's journey.

Measuring the Impact of Integration

To understand the value of your integrated marketing efforts, you need to measure their impact meticulously. It's not just about launching campaigns across various platforms; it's about understanding how these campaigns interact and contribute to your overall goals.

Key Metrics for Integration Success:

- **Customer Engagement:** Track engagement across all platforms. Are customers who interact with your brand on social media also engaging through email or on your website? Increased cross-platform engagement is a good sign of effective integration.
- **Conversion Rates:** Monitor conversion rates from each channel. An uptick in conversions following integrated campaigns can indicate a cohesive strategy that resonates with your audience.
- **Customer Retention:** Integrated marketing aims to create a seamless experience that fosters loyalty. Keep an eye on retention rates; a positive shift suggests your integrated approach is hitting the mark.

Overcoming Integration Obstacles

Integration is not without its challenges, but with the right mindset and strategies, these obstacles can be transformed into opportunities.

Common Integration Hurdles:

- **Data Silos:** Break down data silos by implementing systems that facilitate data sharing and provide a unified view of the customer journey.
- **Resistance to Change:** Change can be daunting. Address this by involving all stakeholders in the planning process and demonstrating the benefits of an integrated approach.

Maintaining Flexibility:

- **Iterative Approach:** Treat integration as an ongoing process. Be ready to iterate and adapt strategies based on performance data and changing market conditions.
- **Training and Support:** Provide teams with the necessary training and resources to navigate new systems and processes effectively.

The Unified Path Forward

The journey toward a fully integrated marketing system is both challenging and rewarding. It's about creating a tapestry of touchpoints that together tell a compelling story about your brand.

Recap of Integrated Marketing Benefits:

- **Cohesive Brand Storytelling:** A unified marketing approach weaves a consistent narrative across all channels, which helps to strengthen your brand identity.

- **Enhanced Customer Experience:** Integration ensures that customers receive a seamless experience, which can enhance satisfaction and loyalty.

A Call to Action:

- **Audit Your Current Systems:** Take stock of your current marketing efforts. Where are the gaps in integration, and what can be improved?
- **Embrace the Integration Journey:** Start small if you need to, but start. The path to integration is a progressive one, with each step building on the last.

By embracing integrated marketing, you're not just streamlining your efforts; you're setting the stage for sustainable growth that resonates with the heart of your customer base. It's a unified path forward, one that promises a more connected and impactful brand presence in the marketplace.

Key Takeaways

- Create a cohesive marketing approach by integrating different aspects of your strategy.

- Ensure alignment between your marketing objectives, tactics, and overall business goals.

- Foster collaboration between different marketing channels for a unified strategy.

- Utilize integrated marketing communications to deliver a consistent brand message across all platforms.

Part IV: Strategies for Transformation

As we embark on the final stretch of this journey together, we arrive at a pivotal crossroads where the past and future of your marketing strategies converge. Part IV is about making that critical turn—from following well-trodden paths to forging your own. It's about recognizing when to bring in expertise and how to transform missteps into milestones.

From Misstep to Milestone: The Pivot Process

Every business, at some juncture, must face the reality that growth requires expertise. It's not just about doing more; it's about doing better—smarter, more strategically.

Here, we'll outline the pivot process, a methodical approach to transforming your marketing to align with your evolving business goals. We'll explore the pros and cons of outsourcing marketing and the common pitfalls of premature delegation. This part of the journey is about recalibration and refinement, ensuring that every step you take is a step toward greater success.

The Marketing Metamorphosis: Tools and Tactics

Transformation is not just a concept; it's a practice. In this segment, we introduce practical tools and tactics that are the building blocks of your marketing metamorphosis. We'll
237

delve into the framework of tools from your marketing toolkit, examining each one for its potential to revolutionize your approach.

The High-Touch in High-Tech Marketing

In the digital age, personal connections can seem like relics of a bygone era. Yet, they remain the heart of successful marketing. We'll dissect how to maintain these high-touch elements within high-tech strategies, showcasing a business that exemplifies excellence in high-touch digital marketing.

Digital Marketing Trends

Finally, we'll cast our gaze forward to the trends that are shaping the entrepreneurial landscape. From the rise of AI to the nuances of voice search and the compelling power of AR/VR content, we'll provide a glimpse into the future, equipping you with knowledge to stay ahead of the curve.

In Part IV, you'll learn not just to adapt to change, but to anticipate and act upon it with precision and purpose. What's in it for you? A transformed marketing approach that's as dynamic and resilient as your business aspirations. Let's pivot process and turn your marketing missteps into milestones.

From Misstep to Milestone: The Pivot Process

Introduction to the Pivot Process

The pivot process stands as a beacon of transformation—a strategic shift in your marketing approach that aligns more closely with the current and future goals of your enterprise. It's not merely a change of direction; it's a calculated repositioning to ensure that your business not only survives but thrives in a competitive market.

Why Pivoting is a Critical Step for Growth

Pivoting is essential for growth because it represents adaptability and resilience. It's the business equivalent of a course correction in navigation, ensuring that you're not just moving, but moving in the right direction.

Growth is not linear; it's an intricate dance of advances, retreats, and side-steps. Pivoting allows you to keep pace with the changing rhythms of the market, customer needs, and technological advancements.

Recognizing the Signs for a Pivot

The signs that a pivot is needed can be as subtle as a gradual decline in customer engagement or as glaring as a significant drop in sales.

- Perhaps your marketing strategies, which once delivered consistent results, are now yielding diminishing returns.
- Or maybe there's a noticeable shift in your industry, and your current methods are becoming obsolete.
- It could also be that your business has outgrown its original marketing strategies, and what worked for a small startup is no longer effective for a growing enterprise.

When you notice these signs, it's not the moment to double down on outdated tactics—it's the call to pivot. By recognizing the need for a pivot, you're taking the first step towards a marketing metamorphosis that can set your business on a new trajectory for success.

In the following sections, we'll delve deeper into the pivot process, exploring how to execute it with precision and how it can serve as a catalyst for your business's growth and evolution.

Marketing Mirror

Reflect on a past marketing misstep. What key
lesson did you learn?

_____

_____

How have you implemented changes based upon
past marketing experiences?

_____

_____

The Expertise Inflection Point

At a certain juncture in a business's growth, the need for
specialized marketing expertise becomes not just an
advantage but a necessity. This pivotal moment can be
described as the 'Expertise Inflection Point'—a stage where
the complexity and scale of marketing efforts surpass the
capabilities of the existing team, necessitating the
integration of external marketing expertise to continue
scaling effectively.

The Benefits of External Marketing Expertise

When you reach the Expertise Inflection Point, bringing in external marketing expertise can be transformative. Here are some of the key benefits:

- **Strategic Insight:** External experts bring a wealth of experience and can offer strategic insights that may not be available internally. They can help set the overall direction for your marketing, ensuring that your efforts are not just tactical but also strategic and aligned with your long-term business goals.
- **Specialized Skills:** Marketing is an ever-evolving field with specialized areas such as digital marketing, SEO, content marketing, and social media. External experts often have specific skills and knowledge in these areas that can be leveraged to gain a competitive edge.
- **Cost Efficiency:** Hiring a full-time, in-house marketing team with the breadth of expertise required can be cost-prohibitive for many businesses. Outsourcing to an agency or consultant can be more cost-effective, allowing you to access a range of skills and experience on a flexible basis.
- **Fresh Perspective:** An external marketing expert can provide a fresh perspective, bringing new ideas and approaches that can revitalize your marketing efforts and help you stand out in the market.

The Challenges of Integrating External Expertise

While the benefits are compelling, integrating external marketing expertise does not come without its challenges:

- **Finding the Right Fit:** It's crucial to find an expert or agency whose approach and values align with your business. This requires careful vetting and clear communication of your needs and expectations.
- **Maintaining Brand Consistency:** There's a risk that external experts may not fully grasp the nuances of your brand voice and values, which can lead to inconsistencies in your marketing materials and campaigns.
- **Knowledge Transfer:** Ensuring that external experts understand your products, services, and market can require significant time and effort in terms of knowledge transfer.
- **Dependency:** Relying on external expertise can sometimes lead to a dependency, which might be risky if the relationship ends. It's important to maintain a balance and ensure knowledge sharing and skills transfer to in-house teams.

Navigating the Decision

Deciding whether to bring in external marketing expertise is a significant one. It's important to evaluate your current marketing goals, understand your branding, and ensure you have the right systems and tools in place before deciding on the level of expertise you need.

Ultimately, the choice to integrate external marketing expertise should be guided by a clear understanding of your business goals, the specific marketing challenges you face, and the level of expertise required to overcome them.

Whether it's hiring a fractional CMO, engaging a marketing agency, or seeking the guidance of a marketing coach, the right external expertise can catalyze growth and lead your business to new heights.

Common Outsourcing Missteps

Outsourcing is a strategic move that can propel a business forward when done correctly. However, it's not without its pitfalls. One of the most common mistakes businesses make is outsourcing tasks before they have a clear strategy in place. It's like putting the cart before the horse—without direction, even the most skilled team can't help you reach your destination.

The Premature Delegation Dilemma

Imagine you're at the helm of a burgeoning enterprise. You've heard that outsourcing can save time and money, so you hire a virtual assistant (VA) to take on the day-to-day marketing tasks. But there's a catch: you haven't fully articulated your brand voice or marketing strategy; and neither you nor the VA have knowledge of other strategies that have seen great results.

This is where the trouble begins.

Your VA is likely competent at executing tasks, but without a clear strategy and aligned communication, those tasks may not align with your business goals. It's akin to speaking a language fluently but having nothing of substance to say.

The result? Your marketing efforts are not only ineffective but could potentially misrepresent your brand.

Case Study: Brand Voice Lost in Translation

Let's consider a real-world scenario. A business owner, let's call her Jane, understood her brand voice in her mind but struggled to communicate it effectively to her VA. She had it in her head, but it wasn't completely clear yet, she would try to explain it to her VA, but it was unclear enough that it didn't click. The result was a disjointed marketing effort that failed to resonate with her audience.

We were speaking for a few minutes offline after I had interviewed her on my podcast, and she was telling me about these issues. I mentioned it's a problem that I see very often in entrepreneurs. Her mistake was not in hiring a VA, but in doing so **before she had solid branding in place** that had been finetuned with the help of an expert. Since we were on video, I could see immediately that a lightbulb went off and I had hit her issue right on the head. She asked to schedule an initial branding session on the spot!

The Strategy Before Task Rule

The key takeaway from Jane's experience is the importance of **strategy before execution**. And no, I am not saying to do nothing until everything is perfect. Before outsourcing, ensure that you have a comprehensive understanding of your marketing goals, target audience, and brand voice. If you don't yet, either do the work to establish those, or take a bit of a shortcut and bring in a pro to help you get there more efficiently.

This foundation is crucial for guiding any freelancers or staff and ensuring that their work contributes to your business's growth.

The Role of a Marketing Expert

A marketing expert, unlike a VA, helps set the overall direction and strategy for your marketing efforts. They bring years of experience and a strategic mindset to the table, ensuring that your marketing is not only efficient but also effective. By first working with an expert to define your marketing strategy, you can then outsource with confidence, knowing that your VA's efforts will be aligned with your business objectives.

Outsourcing too early to a VA is a common misstep that can lead to wasted resources and missed opportunities. By recognizing the importance of a solid marketing strategy and the role of a marketing expert, you can avoid this pitfall and set your business up for success. Remember, it's not just about doing marketing; it's about doing it right.

Strategic Outsourcing Decisions

Outsourcing marketing functions is a significant decision that can lead to substantial growth when executed strategically. The key is to know when and how to delegate these tasks effectively.

When to Outsource: Timing is Everything

We all get SO distracted by the thought that someone can take clerical tasks off our plate that we jump to attention when someone mentions a "VA"! OMG YES as we think of all of the time we can free up in our schedule!

The decision to outsource should come after you've laid a solid foundation for your marketing strategy. This means having a clear understanding of your brand identity, target audience, and the goals you aim to achieve through your marketing efforts. Also an understanding of the strategies that will work not only now, but also as you grow.

Once this is in place, outsourcing can help you scale these efforts efficiently.

How to Outsource: The Right Fit for Your Business

Outsourcing isn't a one-size-fits-all solution; it's about finding the right fit for your business needs. A marketing expert and a virtual assistant serve different purposes:

- **Marketing Expert:** This is a strategist who helps you develop and refine your marketing plan. They provide guidance, accountability, and expertise to help you navigate the marketing landscape and make informed decisions. I serve as the primary expert on my team, with some of my team also assisting their expertise at a strategy level depending upon the project. We help clients define the right strategies.
- **Virtual Assistant:** A VA is more of an executor, someone who takes on specific tasks based on the strategy you've developed. They handle the day-to-day activities that support your marketing initiatives, such as social media posting, email campaign execution, and data entry. The rest of my team is made up of VAs, each with their own specialties, who help in the execution of the strategies.

Making the Choice

Choosing between a marketing expert, such as a Fractional CMO, and a VA depends on where you are in your marketing journey. If you're still defining your strategy, an expert can provide the expertise you need. If you have the right strategy and need help with execution, a VA can take those tasks off your plate.

Step-by-Step Guide to Pivoting Strategies

Pivoting your marketing strategy is a deliberate process that involves assessing what's working, identifying areas for improvement, and implementing changes to better align with your business goals.

Step 1: Assess Your Current Marketing Efforts

Take stock of your current marketing activities. What's yielding results, and what's not? This assessment will form the basis of your pivot.

Step 2: Define Your Pivot Goals

Clearly articulate what you want to achieve with your pivot. Is it increased engagement, higher conversion rates, or entering a new market? Your goals will guide the direction of your pivot.

Step 3: Develop a Strategic Plan

Based on your goals, develop a new marketing strategy. This should include a mix of tactics that are bespoke for your business and target audience.

Step 4: Implement Changes Gradually

Don't try to change everything at once. Implement your new strategies gradually, monitoring results and adjusting as necessary. I like to think of it as layering, especially when you consider that some strategies work best when added on to other strategies and layering them in the right order brings easier and better results.

Step 5: Measure and Adjust

Use metrics to measure the impact of your new strategies. Are you closer to your goals? Use this data to tweak your approach for even better results.

Strategic outsourcing and pivoting your marketing strategies are crucial for growth. By understanding when to outsource and how to pivot effectively, you can ensure that your marketing efforts are both efficient and impactful. Use the provided tools to apply these concepts to your business and watch your marketing transform.

Real-World Examples

The pivot process in marketing is not just a theoretical concept; it's a practical approach that has been the turning point for many businesses. Here are a few real-world examples of companies that have successfully navigated a pivot in their marketing strategies:

- **Buffer**: Initially started as a social media scheduling tool, Buffer pivoted to focus on being a platform for authentic engagement. They shifted their marketing to highlight transparency and build a community, which resonated with their audience and led to sustained growth.

- **Slack**: Slack began as an internal communication tool for a gaming company. When they pivoted to market it as a standalone product for businesses, focusing on improving workplace communication, their user base and revenue skyrocketed.
- **Shopify**: Shopify pivoted from just a tool to sell snowboarding equipment online to a comprehensive e-commerce platform. By broadening their marketing message to empower businesses of all sizes to sell online, they tapped into a much larger market.
- **HubSpot**: Known for inbound marketing, HubSpot made a significant pivot by expanding their marketing to include a full CRM platform. This allowed them to market to a broader audience, including sales teams, and not just marketers.

Each of these companies made strategic changes to their marketing approaches, which resulted in a clear impact on their growth and success.

Embracing the Pivot

The pivot process is a powerful tool in the marketer's arsenal. It's about more than just changing direction; it's about refining and revitalizing your marketing strategy to align with your evolving business landscape. By embracing the pivot, you open up a world of innovation and growth opportunities.

Remember, pivoting isn't a sign of failure; it's a sign of agility and responsiveness to the market. It's about transforming marketing missteps into milestones and seeing every challenge as a chance to innovate. So, take these stories of successful pivots as inspiration and consider how you can apply the pivot process to your own marketing strategies. With the right approach, you can turn what seems like a setback into a setup for your next big success.

Key Takeaways

- Embrace the process of transforming marketing missteps into milestones for growth.

- Learn to identify past marketing mistakes and understand their impact on your business.

- Develop a structured approach to pivot from ineffective strategies to successful ones.

- Implement continuous learning and adaptation as a core part of your marketing strategy.

The Marketing Metamorphosis: Tools and Tactics

Introduction to Marketing Transformation

Embarking on a marketing transformation is akin to a caterpillar's metamorphosis into a butterfly; it's a necessary evolution to ensure survival and success in a business environment that's in constant flux. This transformation isn't just about adopting the latest digital fads or tools; it's a strategic shift in how you approach your audience, craft your message, and deliver value. It's about recognizing the need for change, embracing the process, and emerging more aligned with the needs and behaviors of your customers.

The essence of marketing transformation lies in the ability to not just react to changes but to **anticipate and drive changes**. It's about leveraging the right combination of tools and tactics to create a marketing strategy that's resilient, responsive, and results oriented. It's about understanding that the tools you choose should not only fit your current needs but also scale with your growth.

Tool Overload: Myth vs. Reality

There's sometimes a misconception that success is directly proportional to the number of tools in your arsenal. However, the truth is that the effectiveness of your marketing strategy is not measured by the tools you use, but by how efficiently you use them. It's about selecting tools that offer real value to your business, which integrate well with your existing systems, and that help you streamline your operations.

One of the problems I often see is entrepreneurs who have used different coaches here and there, and purchased some marketing program elsewhere, and used a Fakexpert at some point ... and each one has a tool or platform that you MUST use.

What often happens is the entrepreneur ends up doing *more* work, rather than being *efficient* (which is what technology should actually help you do).

The reality is that **a cluttered toolbox can lead to a cluttered strategy**. It's essential to resist the allure of shiny new tools and focus instead on tools that enhance your ability to communicate with your audience, analyze your data, and automate repetitive tasks. The goal is to create a lean, mean marketing machine that is efficient, effective, and adaptable.

In essence, the journey of marketing transformation is about strategic evolution, not about tool accumulation. It's about making smart choices that empower you to build a marketing strategy that's as dynamic as the marketplace you operate in. Remember, in the world of marketing, sometimes less is indeed more, and simplicity can be the ultimate sophistication.

Essential Tools for Transformation

Let's cut through the noise and focus on what truly matters. When it comes to essential tools for marketing transformation, it's not about having the most, but having the right ones that align with your strategy and goals.

First and foremost, every B2B and B2P business needs a robust **Customer Relationship Management (CRM)** system. A CRM isn't just a fancy database; it's the heartbeat of your customer interactions, tracking every touchpoint and ensuring that nothing falls through the cracks. For service-based B2C businesses, a CRM is equally crucial; although strictly eCommerce B2C can likely use the system's built-in tools. Your CRM is your ally in nurturing leads, delighting customers, and driving growth. (And by robust, I don't mean it has a lot of bells and whistles and is expensive … what it can do needs to align with your needs.)

Then there's your **website**. Yes, even if you're a social media maven with a thriving Facebook community, *you need a website*. It's your digital storefront, open 24/7, **under your control** unlike the ever-changing algorithms of social platforms. It's where you tell your story, showcase your offerings, and convert visitors into customers. Plus, it's one of the few pieces that you have full control over (assuming you aren't using an all-in-one option where you have no access to hosting; don't do that!).

Here's a bullet list of some of the most critical tools:

- **Customer Relationship Management (CRM) System:** The linchpin for managing customer data and interactions.
- **Website:** Your online identity and conversion engine, crucial for all businesses. I always, always recommend that this is NOT on a third-party all-in-one system where you have no control over the hosting and other items.
- **Email Marketing Platform:** For nurturing leads and maintaining customer relationships. This isn't one-to-one email such as Outlook, but sending bulk messages.
- **Analytics Tools:** To measure performance, understand customer behavior, and make data-driven decisions.
- **Content Management System (CMS):** To easily create and manage your website content. Often this will be part of your website (such as WordPress, which is almost always our recommended platform).
- **Social Media Management Tools:** For scheduling posts and managing your presence across platforms.
- **SEO Tools:** To optimize your online content and improve search engine rankings if you're doing it in-house (when outsourcing to experts and they will have their own tools).

Remember, it's not about collecting tools; it's about **selecting the right ones** that serve your business unique needs and help you connect with your audience effectively. It's also about strategically choosing tools that can work together, hopefully seamlessly.

Don't get sidetracked by every new tool that comes your way. Instead, focus on building a solid foundation with tools that support your marketing strategy and enhance your ability to reach and engage your target market.

Case Study: The Chiropractic Conundrum

The Doctor of Chiropractic who owns Spine Wellness Center sought our help after enrolling in a course from an MLM marketing coach. The course mandated the use of a specific marketing system, but the coach was on vacation, and she couldn't set it up on her own.

When I reviewed the system - not just the software platforms but also the overall strategy being used - I quickly realized it posed significant integration challenges with her existing platforms. This disconnection was already resulting in manual data transfer between the existing one and the new one, increasing workload immediately. (I'm a firm believer that technology should work for you, not you having to work at it so hard.)

Initial Strategy Flaws:

1. **Incompatible Systems**: The new system couldn't integrate with her existing tools, leading to redundant work like weekly contact uploads from both systems to the other.
2. **Unproven Efficacy**: The overall strategy had shown limited success with other chiropractors we had worked with upon reviewing similar tactics. It might work a little,

but there were quite a few other options that work better.

Financial Commitment: Dr. Elaine had already invested significantly, both in the coach's fees (high 4-figures) and in buying the new systems, which were an extra $1,000 annually; on top of existing systems she was already using.

Our Approach:

- First, we advised against adopting the strategy as given due to its low ROI and operational inefficiency.
- We provided a candid forecast of the expected results and suggested alternative strategies with better ROI.
- Dr. Elaine did decide to move ahead with the strategy due to the investment she had already made. This is the fallacy of **sunk cost[14].**
- We went ahead and helped her set up her system, since it wasn't entirely negative; and outlined how to use her existing systems in tandem with the new ones as efficiently as possible.

Outcome:

- When we checked in six months later, Dr. Elaine had discontinued the new strategy due to its high effort-to-return ratio.

---

14 Sunk cost fallacy often leads to suboptimal decisions, as seen in Dr. Elaine's case, where an emotional investment in past expenses outweighs rational decision-making based on future outcomes.

- This case highlights our commitment to honest advice; we will not implement strategies that we know generally only offer negative results; and we offer candid insights for those we believe will yield unsatisfactory results.

Key Takeaway: Investing in new strategies requires careful consideration of compatibility with existing systems and proven effectiveness in your specific industry. It's crucial to weigh expert advice against practical applicability and potential ROI.

The Marketing Toolkit Framework

Crafting a personalized marketing toolkit is akin to an artist
selecting the perfect palette for their masterpiece. It's about
choosing the tools that resonate with your brand's vision and
amplify your message. Let's dive into a framework that helps
you evaluate and integrate these tools for maximum
efficiency and impact.

Step 1: Assess Your Needs

Begin by taking stock of where you are and where you want to be. What are your marketing goals? Who is your audience? What's your budget? Your toolkit should be tailored to these factors, ensuring that each tool serves a specific purpose.

Step 2: Audit Your Current Tools

Take a hard look at the tools you're currently using. Are they delivering results? Are they user-friendly? Do they integrate well with each other? This audit will help you identify gaps and redundancies in your existing toolkit.

Step 3: Research and Select Tools

With your goals and current tools in mind, research potential additions to your toolkit. Look for tools that offer the features you need without unnecessary extras that complicate your process. Prioritize tools that offer integration capabilities to ensure a seamless workflow.

Step 4: Test and Evaluate

Before fully committing, test the tools to ensure they meet your expectations. Many tools offer free trials or demo versions. Use this period to evaluate their impact on your marketing efforts.

Step 5: Train Your Team

Once you've selected your tools, ensure your team is well-versed in using them. Proper training can prevent misuse and maximize the potential of each tool in your arsenal.

Step 6: Monitor and Adjust

Your marketing toolkit is not set in stone. Monitor the performance of your tools and be prepared to make adjustments. As your business evolves, so too should your toolkit.

Step 7: Review Regularly

Set a regular schedule to review your toolkit. Marketing technologies evolve rapidly, and staying updated can give you a competitive edge.

By following this framework, you can build a marketing toolkit that is as unique as your business. It's not about having all the tools; it's about having the right tools that work together to create a cohesive and effective marketing machine. Remember, the goal is to achieve Beyond-the-Graph Growth™, where your marketing efforts translate into tangible business success.

Case Studies: Tool Transformation

The adage "work smarter, not harder" is particularly apt in marketing. The following case studies exemplify businesses that have embraced this philosophy by optimizing their marketing toolkits, leading to significant transformations in their operations and outcomes.

Case Study 1: The Chiropractic Clinic's Email Epiphany

Another chiropractor we worked with encountered an email issue.

Harmony Chiropractic & Wellness Center is a bustling chiropractic clinic which had been comfortably using a reliable platform for their email marketing campaigns, and with marked success.

However, upon the advice of a "marketing MLM" coach, they added another platform to their process, a particular "funnel software". This Fakexpert only knew one way to do marketing, and only by using one "funnel" software platform.

This decision, meant to enhance their marketing, instead led to a cumbersome routine of manual data transfer between BOTH platforms, to make sure that any contacts who subscribed to one were added to the other, and those unsubscribed from one were also unsubscribed from the other (an important note to stay on the good side of anti-spam laws.) The new funnel software also cost over $100 per month and had many bells and whistles that they had zero need for in their business (such as website builder; they already had a pretty great website.)

The pivot came when the doctor's staff just got so tired of all of this extra work that they came to me for help. We renovated the strategies suggested by the previous coach but using their existing platforms that they already had in place for years and helped them cancel the other subscriptions. This included hosting things like landing pages on their own website (always sending traffic to your one website is best practice; you never want to split traffic between multiple websites if you can avoid it at all.)

We also tweaked the system that had been suggested by the Fakexpert, since it was a weird strategy for a chiropractor and wasn't working as well as slightly finetuned strategies could. It just wasn't right for their audience. This is a common occurrence with Fakexperts who only know one B2C way to do things, which doesn't work for people like her who actually had B2P clients.

The result? A return to automated simplicity, cut expenses, and a marketing system that was both efficient and effective.

Case Study 2: The Boutique's Digital Makeover

A local accounting company Summit Accounting Solutions, known for its personalized customer service, faced a dilemma. Their marketing tools were a patchwork of applications that didn't communicate, leading to disjointed customer experiences and a taxing workload for the staff.

The transformation began with our 360° Marketing Assessment, which revealed the need for an integrated system. The company transitioned to a CRM that unified their customer interactions, sales data, and email marketing. This shift not only saved hours of manual data entry but also provided a holistic view of their customers' journey, enabling personalized engagements and, ultimately, a boost in customer loyalty and sales.

Case Study 3: The Tech Startup's Resource Reallocation

A tech startup NexGen Innovate Technologies was on the brink of innovation but bogged down by an overabundance of marketing tools to choose from, each promising the moon yet delivering fragmented results. Their marketing efforts were scattered, and the team was overwhelmed.

The startup's pivot was a lesson in resourcefulness. By having the CEO pull back to personally focus on their Zone of Genius, we helped them identify which aspects of marketing were essential to their core operations. With guidance, they curated a suite of tools that not only aligned with their business model but also offered integration, analytics, and automation. This strategic culling of resources redirected their budget from redundant tools to areas that fostered growth, leading to a leaner, more agile marketing approach.

These case studies serve as a testament to the power of strategic tool selection. By choosing the right tools and integrating them into a cohesive system, businesses can transform their marketing efforts from a source of frustration into a streamlined pathway to success. The key lies in understanding your unique needs and making informed decisions that align with your marketing strategy and business goals.

Marketing Automation: Process and Benefits with a Reality Check on AI

For an entrepreneur, time is not just money; it's the lifeblood of business growth and personal freedom. As entrepreneurs, we're often sold the dream of automation as a silver bullet – the one-stop solution that will take marketing off our plates and give us back our time. But let's get real for a moment. While marketing automation is a powerful ally in scaling our businesses, the notion that AI will take over and automate all aspects of marketing is, for now, just that—a notion.

Marketing automation is indeed transformative. It streamlines processes, integrates tasks across platforms, and ensures that your marketing engine runs without constant manual intervention. It's about setting up systems that nurture leads, engage customers, and analyze data while you focus on the bigger picture. But here's the kicker: automation is not a 'set it and forget it' system, especially not when it comes to AI.

The current state of AI in marketing is promising, yet it's not the all-encompassing solution some might hope for. AI can handle tasks like segmenting email lists, personalizing content, or managing some social media posts. It can even offer insights through analytics and reporting. But it's not at a point where it can fully replace the **nuanced and strategic thinking of a human** marketer.

Think of AI as a tool in your marketing toolkit, not the entire box. It's there to enhance your efforts, not to replace the creative and strategic decisions that only you, with your unique understanding of your business, can make. It's about finding that sweet spot where automation supports your work, not overshadows it.

The truth is, even for tech-savvy marketers, AI has not significantly reduced the workload (yet); it has merely **changed the nature of the work**. Instead of freeing up time, many find themselves investing time to learn and manage these new AI tools. And **this particular learning curve is not where you should be focusing your energy as an entrepreneur.** Your 'zone of genius'—that unique value only you bring to your business—should be your priority, not wrestling with the latest AI platform.

So, while AI won't be taking over marketing in the near future, it does offer valuable support. It's about using AI where it makes sense—automating repetitive tasks, providing data-driven insights, and personalizing customer interactions. But it's also about maintaining that personal touch that no algorithm can replicate. Your brand's voice, your strategic vision, and your relationship with customers are irreplaceable by AI.

Marketing automation, augmented by AI, is a process that offers numerous benefits, but it's not a standalone solution. It requires a blend of technology and human insight to truly transform your marketing efforts. Embrace the tools that make sense for your business, but don't lose sight of the human element that makes your brand stand out. Automation is here to serve us, not to replace the irreplaceable.

Tactical Breakdown

In the intricate dance of marketing, each step, each tactic, is a move towards greater engagement and conversion. The right tools don't just make these steps easier; they elevate them to an art form. Let's break down specific tactics that, when paired with the right technological partners, can transform good marketing into great.

Take, for instance, the all-too-common tale of the abandoned shopping cart. It's a frustrating cliffhanger for any e-commerce business: a customer visits, shops, and just before the final click, vanishes. Enter the hero of our story: automated "abandoned cart" emails. Platforms like Mailchimp offer integrations specifically designed for e-commerce websites to address this issue. By connecting your e-commerce platform with an email marketing tool, you can set up a system that automatically reaches out to these near-miss customers. It's a gentle nudge, a reminder of what they've left behind, and it's proven to nudge conversion rates in the right direction.

But it's not just about recovering lost sales; it's about nurturing a relationship. Automated emails can be personalized, offering recommendations based on past browsing or purchase history, creating a bespoke shopping experience that feels less like a marketing ploy and more like a concierge service.

Another tactic where the right tool can make all the difference is in content marketing. Tools that offer content calendar functionalities, like CoSchedule or Asana, or my favorite ClickUp (I have a full content planning and delivery ecosystem set up for me and all of my clients), enable businesses to plan, execute, and track content across multiple channels seamlessly. This strategic planning ensures that your content marketing is consistent, timely, and aligned with your overall marketing goals.

Social media management tools like Hootsuite or Buffer take the guesswork and legwork out of posting schedules, allowing for the bulk scheduling of posts, cross-platform content distribution, and real-time engagement tracking. They turn the chaotic world of social media into a manageable, measurable aspect of your marketing strategy.

Let's not forget about customer relationship management (CRM) systems, which are the backbone of any tactical marketing approach. A robust CRM like Salesforce or HubSpot can track customer interactions, manage leads, and provide data that can be used to personalize the customer journey. It's about having a 360-degree view of your customer, which in turn, allows for highly targeted marketing tactics.

These are just a few examples of how the right tools can enhance specific marketing tactics. Businesses across the spectrum have leveraged integrations and functionalities to great effect. A boutique clothing store might use CRM data to send birthday discounts to loyal customers, while a B2B tech company might use lead scoring within their CRM to prioritize follow-ups by the sales team.

In each case, the tools serve a dual purpose: they automate the mundane, repetitive tasks, freeing up time and creative energy, and they provide a level of personalization and precision that would be nearly impossible to achieve manually. It's this combination that can take your marketing tactics from functional to phenomenal.

Interactive: Toolkit Assessment

To truly harness the power of your marketing toolkit, it's essential to regularly assess its effectiveness and adaptability. Here's a concise, interactive assessment to help you evaluate your current toolkit and identify areas for refinement or upgrade:

Tool Efficiency: Are your current tools reducing time spent on repetitive tasks?
- □ Yes, significantly.
- □ Somewhat, but there's room for improvement.

☐ No, I'm spending as much time as or more than before.

Integration: Do your tools seamlessly integrate with each other, creating a cohesive workflow?

☐ Yes, they work together like a well-oiled machine.

☐ They integrate, but the process isn't smooth.

☐ No, I have to manually bridge the gap between tools.

Data Utilization: Are you able to gather and utilize data effectively for decision-making?

☐ Yes, I have all the data I need at my fingertips.

☐ I get some data, but I'm not sure how to use it effectively.

☐ No, I'm flying blind without useful data.

Customer Experience: Do your tools enhance the customer experience?

☐ Yes, customers have noticed and appreciated the difference.

☐ There's a slight improvement, but it's not game changing.

☐ No, my tools haven't impacted the customer experience.

Scalability: Can your toolkit scale with your business growth?

☐ Yes, it's built to grow with me.

☐ It can handle some growth, but I'll need upgrades soon.

☐ No, I'll need a new toolkit to handle growth.

Based on your responses, here are some steps to consider:

- ☐ If you've checked mostly "Yes", your toolkit is serving you well. Stay informed about new tools that could add even more value.
- ☐ If your responses are mixed, identify the tools that aren't performing and seek alternatives that offer better integration, efficiency, and data analytics.
- ☐ If you've answered "No" to multiple questions, it's time for a toolkit transformation. Prioritize tools that offer integration, scalability, and data-driven insights to elevate your marketing efforts.

Crafting Your Metamorphosis

Your marketing toolkit is more than a set of applications; it's the chrysalis from which your business's marketing metamorphosis emerges. The journey of selecting and utilizing the right tools and tactics is ongoing and dynamic. It requires a mindset that's both adaptable and strategic, one that's open to evolution while grounded in the needs of your business.

As you reflect on the assessment and consider your toolkit, remember that the goal is not just to change but to transform. Transformation implies a profound shift in how you approach marketing, a shift that can lead to remarkable growth and success.

Approach your marketing metamorphosis with curiosity, a willingness to experiment, and a commitment to continuous learning. With the right tools in hand and a strategic mindset, you're not just adapting to the changing landscape of marketing; you're shaping it.

Encourage yourself to be bold in your choices, to embrace the tools that will catapult your marketing from the mundane to the extraordinary. Your business is unique, and your marketing toolkit should reflect that uniqueness. Craft it carefully, tend to it regularly, and watch as your marketing efforts take flight, transforming not just your business but the very way you connect with your customers.

But Wait a Second, Vicky! What's YOUR Tech Stack?

I haven't included mine because it's bespoke to me … just like yours should be bespoke to you!

I've used so, so, so many different software platforms over the years in connection with client projects, I've tested almost all (if not actually all) of them, and I have a few favorites that would work for almost any size of organization. I also have a solid understanding of when one doesn't work, and a different option would be better to achieve a company's goals.

Here's a few of my favorites that work pretty standard across all businesses:

Websites: WordPress, plus WooCommerce if ecommerce is needed. It's an industry standard, it's free, and it's highly extendable that would allow any business to customize their site to allow it to function as deeply as needed.

Task Management: after having used almost every option out there, ClickUp is my favorite and the one I always recommend. I like it better than Asana and Trello and any of the others.

Email Marketing: MailChimp is my go-to. It doesn't have as many unnecessary bells and whistles as others like Constant Contact, and you can add on the extras that you do need.

CRM: I have a couple of different favorites that I recommend to clients depending upon their needs. I use a proprietary one that I've designed for my own use. (I also have other custom tools for my unique use.)

I do have some other tech that would only be needed by a marketer, such as things for SEO, or managing multiple social media clients for example - things not needed by most entrepreneurs.

Other than this, the tech stack that I recommend to any client is as unique as the client, and if they already have platforms in their arsenal then we work with what they have.

Key Takeaways

- Explore and adopt new tools and tactics for a transformative marketing approach.

- Stay abreast of the latest marketing trends and technologies to keep your strategies effective.

- Tailor marketing tools and tactics to fit the unique needs and goals of your business.

- Use a combination of tried-and-true methods and innovative approaches for a balanced strategy.

The High-Touch in High-Tech Marketing

Introduction to High-Touch Digital Marketing

Automation and mass messaging have become the norm, now the concept of high-touch digital marketing emerges as a beacon of personalization. High-touch is about crafting a marketing experience that feels as personal and attentive as a handshake, in a digital world that often feels like a wave from across a crowded room.

Why is this **personal connection** crucial?

Because in a high-tech environment, consumers are bombarded with impersonal ads and automated messages, making genuine human connection a rare commodity. When you focus on high-touch strategies, you're not just another notification on a screen; you become a voice that speaks directly to the individual needs and desires of your audience.

It's about using the tools of technology to build relationships, not just databases.

The Psychology of Connection

The principles of psychology that underpin high-touch marketing strategies are rooted in the basic human need for connection. We are wired to respond to attention, empathy, and genuine interaction. High-touch marketing taps into these instincts by creating strategies that resonate on a personal level, making your audience feel seen and understood.

Digital platforms, often seen as barriers to personal connection, can actually be powerful conduits for emotional resonance when used thoughtfully. They offer myriad ways to tailor messages, remember preferences, and respond to feedback in real-time. By leveraging these capabilities, you can transform a digital platform from a cold touchpoint into a warm handshake, fostering a sense of belonging and community that resonates deeply with your audience.

Marketing Mirror

How do you maintain a personal touch in your marketing amidst increasing technological advancements?

Can you think of an instance where technology either enhanced or hindered the personal connection with your audience?

High-Touch in High-Tech Marketing: Balancing Your Approach

- Review each pair in the table.
- Assess whether your current marketing strategies effectively balance high-tech tools with high-touch approaches.
- Identify areas where you could enhance the personal touch to balance technological advancements.

High-Tech Elements	High-Touch Counterparts
Automated Email Campaigns	Personalized Email Signatures and Humanized Content
Social Media Algorithms	Engaging Directly with Followers in Comments and Messages
Data-Driven Targeting	Empathetic Messaging that Resonates with Audience Needs
AI Chatbots for Customer Service	Availability of Human Support for Complex Queries
Programmatic Advertising	Storytelling and Authentic Brand Narratives

Web Analytics	Customer Surveys and Direct Feedback Mechanisms
Online Transaction Processes	Personalized Thank You Messages or Follow-ups
CRM Software	Building Personal Relationships and Understanding Customer Histories

Strategies for Emotional Engagement

To forge a genuine connection with your audience, your marketing messages must resonate emotionally. Emotional engagement is the secret sauce that transforms passive observers into active participants, advocates, and loyal customers. Here's some ways you can infuse your marketing with the kind of emotional intelligence that turns heads and wins hearts:

- **Personalization at First Sight:** From the moment a prospect encounters your brand, whether it's a social media ad or a website visit, greet them with personalization (this isn't always as easy for solo entrepreneurs and small teams, but implement when you can). Use data intelligently to address them by name, to make recommendations based on past interactions, or tailor content to their location or browsing history.

- **Empathy in Communication:** Show that you understand and care about your customers' challenges and aspirations. Craft messages that speak directly to their pain points and how your product or service provides relief or a path to their goals.

- **Storytelling with Substance:** Every brand has a story, but the magic lies in telling it in a way that your audience sees themselves as the protagonist. Share customer success stories, behind-the-scenes glimpses, and narratives that highlight the human element of your brand.

- **Consistency Across Channels:** Ensure that the emotional tone of your messaging is consistent across all platforms. Whether it's the warmth of your welcome email or the friendliness of your social media posts, maintain a tone that's unmistakably you. I'm not saying to "be emotional" but your storytelling should evoke emotions in your audience.

- **Interactive and Responsive Design:** Create interactive experiences on your digital platforms that invite participation. Use responsive design to ensure that your website or app responds to user actions in a way that feels intuitive and engaging.

- **Real-Time Reactions:** Utilize chatbots and social media to provide immediate responses to customer inquiries. When customers feel heard and attended to without delay, it builds trust and strengthens the emotional bond.

- **Content that Resonates:** Develop content that strikes a chord with your audience's values and interests. Whether it's a blog post, a video, or an infographic, make sure it's something that they'll find useful, entertaining, or inspiring.
- **Surprise and Delight:** Go beyond expectations with unexpected gestures that make customers feel special. This could be a personalized thank you note, a birthday discount, or a feature on your customer in your newsletter.

By implementing these strategies, you'll ensure that every touchpoint with your brand is not just a transaction but a step in building a meaningful relationship that stands the test of time and technology.

Case Study: The Goat That Made Me Want to Buy a $75 Sweater

The power of a well-crafted story can be the catalyst for a brand's success. Let's delve into a case study that exemplifies the art of storytelling through video to drive sales, without directly referencing the source material.

The Narrative That Captured Hearts

Imagine a brand that has taken the essence of its product and woven a narrative so compelling that it not only informs but also entertains and resonates with its audience on an emotional level. Naadam used the medium of video[15] to not just showcase a product, but to tell a story that embodies the journey and the values behind it.

The Opening Scene

The video opens with breathtaking visuals, transporting viewers to the vast, rugged landscapes where the journey begins. Instead of a direct sales pitch, the brand opts for a narrative that immerses the viewer in the culture and origins of the product. This approach is refreshing and bold, setting the brand apart from its competitors.

Engaging the Viewer

As the story unfolds, the brand cleverly integrates humor and lifestyle elements that align with their audience's values and interests. This isn't just about selling a product; it's about sharing a lifestyle and a set of values that the brand and its customers hold dear.

The Message

Throughout the video, the brand maintains a fast pace, ensuring that the viewer's attention is captured from start to finish. They share only what's essential, allowing the story to breathe and the product's quality and ethical production

---

15 You can watch this video yourself at https://youtu.be/_a_DPZG5xkc

practices to shine through without overwhelming the audience with information.

The Impact

The result is a masterclass in visual storytelling that leaves the viewer not just informed but connected to the brand on a deeper level. It's a testament to the brand's understanding of its audience and the power of storytelling in marketing.

The Takeaway

What we learn from this case study is the importance of knowing your audience and refining your brand to communicate your values effectively. A story well told can transcend the traditional boundaries of marketing, creating a bond between the brand and the consumer that is both memorable and impactful.

Crafting Your Narrative

While not every business has access to the same level of resources to make the type of professional polished video that this business created (and you don't need to - that's another common misconception), the principles of storytelling remain the same. Know your audience, keep it engaging, focus on what matters, and let your brand's values lead the narrative. Whether it's through humor, emotion, or sheer creativity, your story can leave a lasting impression that goes beyond the product itself.

This case study serves as an inspiration for brands looking to harness the power of storytelling in their marketing efforts. It's a reminder that at the heart of every product is a story waiting to be told, and when done right, it can transform the mundane into the extraordinary, driving sales and building a loyal customer base.

Sensory Marketing in a Digital World

Sensory marketing often seems like a concept reserved for brick-and-mortar experiences. However, with a bit of creativity, the sensory appeal can be translated into the digital space, engaging customers in a multi-dimensional way.

Audio Elements: More Than Just Background Noise

Consider the power of audio. Just as Christmas music can instantly transport someone into a festive headspace, compelling auditory elements on a website or in an advertisement can evoke powerful emotions and memories. The strategic use of sound can create an atmosphere that complements the visual message, reinforcing brand identity and enhancing the user experience.

Even online, you can use audio to evoke emotions. For instance, a website selling beach vacations might feature the soothing sounds of waves and seagulls, while a video for a luxury car dealer could incorporate the revving of an engine to evoke power and precision. These sounds can trigger emotional responses and memories, making the digital experience more immersive. Like all things, it needs to be well thought out before implementation … it's not always the right thing to do.

Visual Storytelling: Painting Pictures with Purpose

Visual elements, too, play a crucial role in sensory marketing. The right imagery can tell a story without words, conveying messages that resonate on a deeper level. High-quality images, engaging videos, and interactive graphics can all be used to create a sensory-rich experience online.

A visually stunning campaign can capture the essence of a brand's story, much like a well-decorated mall sets the scene for holiday shopping. The key is to create visuals that not only look good but also feel personal and relatable, encouraging customers to form a connection with the brand. This doesn't mean you need to spend a lot on production. It's actually not as important for the image or video to be aesthetically perfect as it is for them to be **authentic** and tell the right **story**.

High-Touch Tactics in the Digital Marketing Mix

High-touch tactics in digital marketing are about creating personal connections and delivering memorable experiences. Here are practical examples of how businesses can implement these strategies to enhance their digital campaigns.

Personalized Experiences: From First Click to Lasting Impression

Creating personalized experiences is at the heart of high-touch digital marketing. This can range from addressing customers by name in emails to offering personalized product recommendations on a website. By leveraging data and customer insights, businesses can tailor their digital touchpoints to feel more intimate and relevant to each individual.

Leveraging Social Proof: The Power of Community

Social proof is a potent tool in the digital space. Showcasing customer testimonials, user-generated content, and influencer partnerships can build trust and credibility. When potential customers see others enjoying a product or service, it creates a sense of community and belonging, encouraging them to join in.

Exclusivity and Urgency: VIP Treatment Online

Offering exclusive deals or time-sensitive promotions can create a sense of urgency and exclusivity. This tactic taps into the psychological principle of scarcity, making customers feel they are part of a select group with access to special opportunities.

Seamless Shopping: The Convenience Factor

Nowadays convenience is king. Ensuring that your website is easy to navigate, mobile-friendly, and offers hassle-free payment options can significantly enhance the customer experience. The easier it is for customers to find what they need and complete a purchase, the more likely they are to return.

Engaging Content: Educate, Entertain, Inspire

Finally, content that educates, entertains, or inspires can be a powerful high-touch tactic. Whether it's a blog post, a how-to video, or an interactive quiz, providing value beyond the product itself can foster a deeper connection with the audience.

By integrating these high-touch tactics into your digital marketing strategy, you can create a more engaging and emotionally resonant experience for your customers, leading to stronger relationships and, ultimately, better business results.

Maintaining the Human Element

It's crucial to remember that marketing, at its core, is about human connection. As we embrace the convenience of technology, we must be vigilant not to lose the human element that fosters genuine relationships with our audience.

Personalization is Key

One way to maintain the human touch is through **personalization**. Use data not just to target but to understand and connect with your audience on a deeper level. Personalized content, tailored to individual preferences and behaviors, can make your audience feel seen and valued.

Empathy in Automation

Even automated messages can and should be **empathetic**. They can be crafted in a way that feels personal and considerate, rather than robotic and cold. For instance, chatbots can be programmed with a variety of responses to more closely mimic human interaction, making the customer feel heard and assisted.

Community Engagement

Fostering a sense of **community** is another powerful way to keep the human touch alive. Encourage conversations around your brand on social media, create forums for discussion, and actively participate in these spaces to show that there are real people behind the digital facade.

Interactive: Emotional Impact Assessment

To help you gauge the emotional resonance of your marketing efforts, consider this simple assessment tool. Reflect on your current strategies and ask yourself:

- ☐ Do my marketing messages evoke the feelings I intend?
- ☐ Have I received feedback that suggests an emotional connection with my brand?
- ☐ Are there opportunities to add more personalized touches to my digital interactions?

Use these insights to infuse your digital marketing with elements that appeal to the emotions, ensuring that every touchpoint feels personal and impactful.

As we wrap up this exploration of high-touch digital marketing, remember that the goal is not to choose between technology and personal connection but to find the sweet spot where they work in harmony. High-tech can amplify high-touch, leading to a marketing strategy that is both efficient and emotionally resonant.

Embrace the tools and technologies available, but use them to enhance, not replace, the personal interactions that build lasting relationships with your customers. By integrating high-touch strategies into your digital marketing, you create a presence that is not only compelling but also profoundly human.

Case Study: The High-Touch Digital Connoisseur

Consider the case of a boutique local hotel - Serenity Haven Hotel - that mastered the art of high-touch digital marketing. They used customer data to provide personalized room preferences and local experience recommendations.

Their social media platforms were a hub of interaction, where they responded to each review and comment with a personal touch, making guests feel part of their community. They leveraged technology to enhance the customer experience, not to overshadow the personal connections that their brand was built upon. This approach not only increased customer loyalty but also set them apart in a highly competitive market.

Key Takeaways

- Blend high-tech solutions with a high-touch, personalized approach for maximum impact.

- Leverage technology to enhance customer experience while maintaining a personal connection.

- Utilize digital tools to streamline processes without losing the human element in marketing.

- Balance automation and personalization to create effective and efficient marketing campaigns.

Digital Marketing Trends

Introduction to Modern Marketing Trends

You've seen it, haven't you? The digital marketing landscape isn't just changing; it's evolving at *warp speed*. Keeping up can feel like you're running a marathon with the finish line constantly moving further and further away.

But here's the thing: staying ahead of trends isn't just about keeping pace; it's about anticipating the shifts and *using them to your advantage*.

Let's talk about a few of the big players on the field right now: AI, voice search, and video content. Sometimes all three combined. (And knowing the speed at which technology changes things, by the time you get this book in your hands, even as quickly as a month after I'm finished writing, there could be ten more!)

These aren't just buzzwords; they're the tools reshaping the way we connect with our audience. AI is like the new intern that works 24/7; AI along with voice search is changing the SEO game, and video content? It's the billboard that everyone's actually stopping to look at.

But here's where many entrepreneurs trip up: they jump on these trends like they're lifeboats in the open sea, often without a compass. A new shiny tool MUST be *the thing* that makes a difference, right? SQUIRREL!

And believe me, between the time I write this, and the time you read it, there could be 10 or 100 or 1000 new shiny trends to entice you. But **which one is right for your business**?

The key isn't to just use these tools, but to understand how they fit into your unique business puzzle. That's where the pivot happens—from trend-chasing to trend-optimizing.

Artificial Intelligence in Marketing

Now, let's zero in on AI. It's not just a futuristic concept; it's
here, and it's ready to work for you. Think of AI as your
right-hand man in marketing. From customer service
chatbots that never sleep to personalized marketing efforts
that make your customers feel like you're speaking directly
to them, AI is the personal assistant we've all dreamed of.

295

But, and this is a big but, it's not about letting AI run the show. The most common misstep? Thinking AI can replace the human touch. It can't. What it can do is enhance the experience. It's the balance between automation and personalization where AI shines. It's about using AI to handle the data and grunt work so you can focus on what you do best—connecting with your customers on a human level.

AI in marketing is like salt in cooking; used wisely, it enhances the flavors, but overdo it, and you'll spoil the dish. The pivot here is understanding that AI is a tool, not a replacement. It's about using AI to amplify your strengths, not overshadow them.

But wait, Vicky … how do YOU use AI in marketing?

Ah … the burning question, how do I use AI as a marketer? I have found it's helpful with some specific things like:

- Creating fictional names for case studies to maintain client confidentiality. I don't need to think, just pop in a paragraph or so from the study and it just as quickly pops out a fictional name.
- Brainstorming ideas as an additional "brain" for solo work sessions. Two brains are always better than one!
- Writing outlines, followed by my manual revisions for fine-tuning. I don't have it do my final writing as it can't

provide personal anecdotes and case studies, and often feels stiff.

- Revising awkward or choppy paragraphs I have manually written to enhance readability.

- Reviewing programming code to quickly identify errors like extra commas. I really hate those extra commas, and AI can usually (but not always) find them quicker.

- Summarizing large amounts of data, such as extracting common themes from a group of my blog posts or competitor analysis.

- Compiling recipes and generating combined grocery lists for personal use. I've created my own (vegetarian) prompt and do this weekly.

- Drafting email responses based on given context (the email I'm replying to) and key points that need to be included in my response, but also avoiding confidential information (because it's not confidential once you paste it into an AI platform).

- Finding stats about a specific topic, always requesting the source link, and then I manually verify for accuracy and that the link is functional.

- Sometimes for creating an image, if I don't mind that it looks like it was done by AI.

I keep in mind that AI is a language processing tool, always cross-checking for accuracy and appropriateness. It doesn't think, it simply supplies the next word in a sentence that would be most likely to be written, and then the next sentence in the paragraph. AI is a supportive tool rather than a standalone solution.

Voice Search Optimization

Imagine this: a potential customer is cooking dinner, their hands are full, but they need your services. They turn to their voice assistant and ask where they can find what you offer. This is where voice search optimization becomes your new best friend. It's not just about typing on keyboards anymore; it's about being the answer to the question they ask aloud.

The rise of voice search is transforming SEO and content marketing in ways we hadn't imagined a decade ago. The key to staying competitive? Speak their language. Literally. Your content needs to be conversational, natural, and precisely the answer they're looking for. Think about the questions your customers are asking and how they're asking them. Your content should be the conversation that starts with "Hey, Google" and ends with your brand name.

But here's the pivot point: many businesses cram keywords into their content, hoping to rank higher. That hasn't worked for over a decade. The smarter move? Focus on questions that mirror natural speech and provide the answer. This isn't just about being found; it's about being the obvious choice when the answer is spoken back to them.

The Video Content Post-Revolution

Now, let's switch gears to video content. It's been around a long, long time, yet many entrepreneurs still aren't using it to its full potential. And like all things, it may not be a strategy that's right for your business just because it worked for someone else.

If a picture is worth a thousand words, a video is worth a million. Video content is the revolution that's already here, yet it's still also on the growing phase as businesses continue to explore and adopt. It's the tool that can capture attention, convey emotion, and create a lasting impression all within a few minutes or even seconds.

But as you've probably seen, not all video content is created equal. The secret sauce? It's not just about high production value; it's about storytelling and authenticity. Your video content should tell a story that resonates with your target audience, one that they want to be a part of. It's about creating an experience rather than just broadcasting a message.

The common misstep here is producing video for the sake of video. The pivot? Crafting **video content with intention**. Videos should be strategic, with a clear message that aligns with your brand values and speaks directly to the desires and needs of your audience. It's not just about going viral; it's about creating value that sticks.

Augmented and Virtual Reality

Augmented Reality (AR) and Virtual Reality (VR) are not just for gamers and tech enthusiasts anymore; they're becoming a marketer's dream. I'm a huge fan, and actually get my workout in VR in my Oculus headset with Supernatural.

These technologies are the bridge between high-tech capabilities and high-touch experiences, offering a new realm of customer engagement, and I've already been exploring them for a few years.

Imagine your customers not just looking at a product online but experiencing it in their space with AR or walking through a virtual event with VR. This isn't the future; it's the now. Amazon and other big online retailers are already doing this with household items like furniture (and it will be easier for you to do soon enough.)

The practical applications of AR and VR in marketing are vast. Retailers are using AR to let customers try before they buy, from seeing how furniture fits in their living room to trying on clothes virtually. Real estate agents offer virtual tours, allowing potential buyers to walk through a property from anywhere in the world. These experiences are not just novel; they're becoming expected.

But here's where some businesses get it wrong: they use AR and VR as *gimmicks*, flashy tech with no substance. The pivot is to use these tools to solve real customer problems, to enhance their buying journey, and to give them a taste of what's to come. It's about using technology to create connections, not just impressions.

I've been playing with fun ways that even a solo entrepreneur might be able to implement some of these strategies into their marketing mix without costing a lot of time or money.

Like all marketing strategies, just because it exists doesn't mean you must use it. There are likely other strategies that you should consider for your business first.

The Automation Question: Balancing Efficiency with Empathy

Automation in digital marketing is a double-edged sword. On one side, it promises unparalleled efficiency, the ability to reach more people with less effort. On the other, it threatens the personal touch that brands have worked so hard to cultivate. The question isn't whether to automate; it's how to do it without losing the essence of your brand.

The concern with automation is that it can lead to a *one-size-fits-all approach*, where personalized experiences are sacrificed for the sake of scale. However, when done right, automation can free up your time to do more of what only you can do—create and nurture genuine connections with your customers.

The key is to find the balance. Use automation to handle the repetitive tasks but keep the human element in the interactions that matter. Automated emails can alert customers to new products, but personalized follow-ups on their experience can make all the difference. Chatbots can answer FAQs, but they should hand them off to a human when a customer's needs become complex.

In marketing, as in all things, it's about finding harmony between the innovative and the timeless—between the cutting-edge tools that technology offers and the age-old art of human connection.

Interactive: Trend Adoption Checklist

I'm here to help you overcome shiny object syndrome.

When considering the adoption of new digital marketing trends, it's crucial to ensure they align with your business goals and capabilities. This checklist will help you assess the suitability of each trend for your business and determine your readiness for implementation.

Business Alignment and Goals
- ☐ Does the trend align with my business's core values and brand message?
- ☐ Will this trend help me reach my specific business goals (e.g., increasing engagement, boosting sales)?
- ☐ Have I identified clear objectives for what I want to achieve by adopting this trend?

Customer Experience and Engagement
- ☐ Will this trend enhance the customer experience in a way that's meaningful to my target audience?

- Does it have the potential to increase customer engagement and retention?
- Can this trend provide a more personalized experience for my customers?

Technical Readiness

- Do I have the necessary technology infrastructure to implement this trend?
- Is my team equipped with the skills required to utilize this technology effectively?
- If not, am I prepared to invest in training or hiring to fill this gap?
- Is it duplicating something we already have and use?

Resource Assessment

- Have I evaluated the cost versus the potential ROI of adopting this trend?
- Do I have the budget to invest in this technology without hindering other critical business operations?
- Are there resources (time, personnel, money) available to maintain the technology once it's implemented?

Competitive Advantage

- Will adopting this trend give me a competitive edge in my industry?
- Is this trend widely used by my competitors, or is it a unique opportunity for differentiation?

Scalability and Growth

- Can this trend grow and scale with my business?
- Is the trend adaptable to the future changes and directions my business might take?

Risk Management

- ☐ Have I considered the potential risks of adopting this trend (e.g., privacy concerns, brand misalignment)?
- ☐ Do I have a plan to mitigate these risks?

Long-Term Viability

- ☐ Is this trend likely to be long-lasting, or could it be a passing fad?
- ☐ How will this trend evolve, and am I prepared to adapt to its changes?

By thoroughly evaluating each of these areas, you can make an informed decision about which digital marketing trends are worth pursuing for your business. Remember, it's not about jumping on every bandwagon but about choosing the right vehicles to drive your business forward.

Case Studies: Trendsetters in Action

In the landscape of digital marketing, some businesses stand out as pioneers, integrating advanced trends like AR/VR to not only dazzle consumers but also to drive tangible business results. Let's explore a couple of case studies that showcase the successful application of these trends and extract lessons for smaller entrepreneurs.

IKEA: Democratizing Interior Design with AR

IKEA, the Swedish furniture giant, has long been at the forefront of leveraging technology to enhance customer experience. Their AR app, IKEA Place, allows users to

304

visualize how furniture would look and fit in their own space before making a purchase. This use of AR technology solves a real-world problem—will this sofa fit in my living room?—and turns it into an engaging, interactive customer experience.

Outcomes:

- Can increase customer confidence, leading to higher sales.
- Reduction in returns and exchanges due to incorrect sizing or style mismatches.
- Enhanced brand engagement and customer satisfaction.

Lessons for Entrepreneurs:

- Focus on AR/VR solutions that solve a specific problem for your customers.
- Ensure that the technology is accessible and adds value to the customer journey.
- Start small; you don't need an option for *every* product, perhaps begin with your bestsellers.

Sephora: Virtual Try-Ons Transforming Beauty Shopping

Sephora's Virtual Artist app uses AR technology to allow customers to see how makeup products will look on their face before they make a purchase. By turning the camera into a virtual mirror, customers can try on different shades and styles in real-time, making the online shopping experience as tactile as the in-store one.

- Boosts online engagement and sales.
- Reduces hesitation in purchasing makeup online, a traditionally 'try before you buy' market.
- Gathers valuable data on consumer preferences and trends.

Lessons for Entrepreneurs:

- Use AR to bridge the gap between online and offline experiences.
- Collect data to understand your customers better and personalize their experiences.
- Remember, simplicity is key; the app should be intuitive and easy to use.

The Big Mistake: Overcomplicating for the Sake of Flash

A common misstep for entrepreneurs is getting entangled in complex technologies that look impressive but are misaligned with their business goals or customer needs.

An example is a small boutique attempting to create a fully immersive VR store experience without considering if their target market has access to or interest in using VR headsets.

Outcomes:

- Wasted resources on technology with low adoption rates among their customer base.

- Neglected other areas of the business that could provide more ROI, like SEO or email marketing.

Lessons for Entrepreneurs:

- Align technology investments with your customer's habits and preferences.
- Don't let the allure of new trends overshadow the fundamentals that drive your business.
- Implement scalable innovations that can grow with your business and customer base.

By examining real-world applications, smaller businesses can glean that the key is not to replicate these strategies wholesale but to distill the essence of what makes them successful: solving a customer problem, enhancing the buying experience, and ensuring the technology is a natural fit for the brand and its consumers. It's about smart integration, not just flashy innovation.

Looking Ahead: The Future of Digital Marketing

As we peer into the horizon of future digital marketing, the landscape is vibrant with potential. Artificial Intelligence is expected to become even more intuitive, perhaps even predicting consumer behavior before the consumers themselves are aware of their needs. Voice search will likely continue to refine its accuracy, becoming a seamless part of daily life. Video content, already a titan in the marketing world, may evolve into even more interactive forms, possibly integrating live elements to foster real-time engagement.

Predictions for the Road Ahead:

- **Hyper-Personalization:** AI could tailor marketing experiences not just to segments, but to individuals, crafting unique narratives for each consumer.
- **Voice as the New Touch:** Voice search may become the primary mode of interaction, reducing screen time and making 'voice the new touch'.
- **Interactive Video:** Video content might offer viewers the ability to interact with the story, choosing their own paths and outcomes.

New Trends on the Horizon:

- **Sensory Marketing in Digital:** Advancements in technology may allow brands to engage other senses, like smell and touch, even in digital marketing.
- **Decentralized Marketing:** Blockchain could introduce a new era of transparency and consumer control over personal data, changing how marketers approach their audience.

Entrepreneur Takeaway:

Stay curious and agile. The future is not written; it's created by those who dare to innovate and adapt. Keep learning and be ready to pivot to the next big thing.

Riding the Trend Wave

In the ebb and flow of digital marketing trends, the key is not just to ride the wave but to do so with intention and strategy. Much like a surfer finding just the right wave.

We've seen how AI, voice search, video content, and immersive technologies like AR and VR are not just passing fads but significant shifts in the marketing paradigm.

As you stand at the cusp of these exciting times, let these insights be your guide. Consider how each trend can serve your unique narrative, how it can amplify your voice in the marketplace, and how it can elevate your customer's experience. Embrace the trend wave with both foresight and wisdom, and let it propel you toward growth and enduring relevance in the digital age.

Key Takeaways

- Stay updated on current digital marketing trends to keep your strategies relevant and effective.

- Analyze and incorporate trends that align with your business objectives and audience preferences.

- Be cautious of fads and focus on trends with long-term potential for your business.

- Continuously evaluate the effectiveness of adopted trends and be ready to adapt as necessary.

Part V: Sustaining Success

As we embark on Part V of our marketing odyssey, we reach the stage where the fruits of our labor begin to ripen. This is the realm of sustained success, where patience becomes a virtue and perseverance becomes your most trusted ally. Here, we'll explore the principles that ensure your marketing efforts not only take root but flourish over time.

The Rule of 7: Patience and Perseverance

There's a magic number that often gets overlooked in the world of marketing: seven. It's not about instant gratification but the power of persistence and the impact of your message over time. We'll delve into the 'Rule of 7', understanding why your marketing message needs to be heard repeatedly to resonate with your audience.

This section will unravel the threads of consistency and the patience required to see your strategies bear fruit. I'll share a personal story where playing the long game with my marketing efforts led to a payoff that was both satisfying and affirming. It's a narrative that underscores the value of steadfastness in a world that often chases after the new and the now.

Beyond the Million Dollars: Long-Term Marketing Strategies

Reaching your initial goals is a milestone, but what comes next? How do you ensure that your success is not a fleeting moment but a steppingstone to greater achievements? This section is dedicated to the strategies that help you maintain momentum and scale your success. We'll examine the journey of a business that didn't just reach its targets but soared beyond them, setting new benchmarks along the way. It's a testament to the power of long-term planning and the strategic foresight that positions a business for continuous growth.

In Part V, you'll learn the art of marketing endurance and the strategies that sustain success over the long haul. What's in it for you? A blueprint for building a marketing legacy that lasts, the wisdom to know when to hold steady and when to evolve, and the vision to see beyond the horizon of your current achievements. Let's embrace the steady beat of progress and march towards a future where your marketing not only survives but thrives.

The Rule of 7: Patience and Perseverance

Understanding the 'Rule of 7'

There's a seasoned traveler that has been through the twists and turns of consumer behavior: the 'Rule of 7'. This principle suggests that a potential customer *needs to encounter your marketing message* **at least seven times** before they take notice. It's a journey of familiarity, where each touchpoint is a step closer to trust and action.

The 'Rule of 7' is not a one-size-fits-all; it's more of a tailored suit, fitting differently based upon your product, service, and audience. But it's a reliable compass for navigating the marketing landscape. Whether it's through a schedule of emails over a month or a consistent social media ad campaign, the key is persistence and consistency. It's about creating a rhythm in your messaging that aligns with the beat of your customer's daily life.

Where so many entrepreneurs go wrong is sharing a message once, sometimes **only once**, and when it hasn't immediately driven results, switch to something else.

Social media, the bustling marketplace of the digital age, is a fertile ground for applying the 'Rule of 7'. Here, you can craft a content calendar that peppers your message across the week, or you can target your ideal customer with ads that gently nudge them towards your brand. The goal is to become a familiar face in a crowd of strangers.

But does this mean repeating the same message verbatim? **Absolutely**. I'm not saying to have ONLY one message. It's about carving your message into the digital landscape, ensuring it's seen across various platforms and times. Like a favorite song on the radio, it's the *repetition that breeds familiarity* and eventually, **affinity**[16].

Yet, there's a delicate dance to this strategy. It's not about overwhelming your audience with a relentless echo but about strategically placing your message, so it feels like a natural part of their digital journey. Think of it as a breadcrumb trail leading them to your door, not a barrage that drives them away.

In essence, the 'Rule of 7' is about crafting a narrative that weaves through the customer's daily life, becoming a part of their story. It's a reminder that in the bustling world of marketing, it's the familiar tales that capture hearts and minds.

---

16 Beyond just connection, affinity is a sense of fondness or liking that develops over time. It refers to the emotional connection and positive association that customers gradually build towards a brand or message, often as a result of consistent and familiar exposure. In marketing, this affinity is crucial as it leads to brand loyalty and preference.

Consistency in Messaging

Consistency is the drumbeat of your brand's heart. It's the steady pulse that resonates across the diverse landscape of marketing channels, from the vibrant visuals of Instagram to the professional handshake of LinkedIn. But let's clear the air: consistency isn't about standing still. It's about evolving while holding on to the core voice that defines your brand.

The misconception that consistency leads to stagnation is a trap that ensnares many. In reality, it's the golden thread that ties together the tapestry of your marketing efforts. It's about delivering a coherent message that adapts to the platform while retaining its essence. This is not a call to monotony but a rally to harmonize your brand's voice across the symphony of channels.

Consider the changing seasons: the essence of nature remains, even as it dons different leaves. Your brand should mirror this natural cycle, shifting its strategies without losing its identity. It's about being recognizable, whether you're whispering through email or shouting from billboards.

Pivoting doesn't mean losing your way; it's about finding new paths while leaving a trail of breadcrumbs that leads back to you. It's about being the North Star in the ever-shifting skies of the market: a constant, reliable presence that guides your audience home.

In the end, consistency in messaging is about trust. It's about building a bridge of familiarity that can weather the storms of market changes. It's about being a beacon of stability in the ever-changing tides of consumer interests. So, pivot with purpose, evolve with elegance, and let your consistent message be the lighthouse that guides your customers to shore.

Strategic Patience in Marketing

It's easy to fall into the trap of constant change when so much of the business world is flying by so fast, believing that the next big pivot will be the one that catapults your business to success. SQUIRREL!

However, this approach can often lead to a cycle of short-term tactics that fail to yield long-term results. The truth is, marketing strategies are more akin to a fine wine—they need time to mature and develop to truly show their worth.

The allure of immediate results can be tempting, but it's a siren call that leads many entrepreneurs astray.

Consider the advice I gave one client who asked about changing their email newsletter monthly. Isn't that what they should be doing so that it *always looks fresh*?

While it may seem like a good idea on the surface to keep things new and exciting, this can actually disorient and frustrate your audience, much like the annoyance of finding your favorite snack moved around the grocery store each visit. (So annoying!) **Consistency** (in this case by using a standard template) **breeds familiarity**, and familiarity breeds trust—a crucial ingredient in the relationship between you and your audience.

The key is to give your strategies time to breathe, to collect data, and to see the patterns of what truly resonates with your audience. It's not about being static; it's about being strategic. When you do decide to make changes, they should be informed by data and driven by a clear benefit to your customer, not just a knee-jerk reaction to a perceived lack of engagement.

Marketing Mirror

Can you recall a marketing effort that required more patience and perseverance than you initially expected? How did it turn out?

_____

_____

_____

How do you currently measure the success of long-term marketing strategies in your business?

_____

_____

_____

Patience and Perseverance: Self-Reflection

Evaluating Expectations vs. Reality: Reflect on a time when a marketing strategy took longer than expected to yield results. What were your initial expectations, and how did they compare to the actual outcomes?

Understanding the Journey: Think about the process of developing and implementing a long-term marketing strategy. What challenges did you face, and how did you overcome them?

Measuring Success Over Time: How do you evaluate the success of your marketing strategies over extended periods? What metrics or indicators do you use?

Adapting to Changes: Consider how you have adapted your marketing strategies in response to unexpected market changes or challenges. How did these adaptations affect the overall outcome?

Learning from the Process: What have you learned about patience and perseverance from your past marketing efforts? How has this influenced your current or future strategies?

Resource Management: Reflect on how you allocate resources (time, budget, manpower) for long-term versus short-term marketing strategies. How do you ensure these resources are used effectively over time?

Balancing Persistence with Flexibility: How do you balance being persistent with a strategy and being flexible enough to pivot when necessary?

Personal Anecdote: The Rewards of Resilience

Let me share a story from my own marketing journey that underscores the power of patience. There was a time when I was managing a campaign that, despite all efforts, wasn't performing as expected. The pressure to pivot was immense, but instead of scrapping everything, I decided to dig deeper into the data, to understand the 'why' behind the 'what.'

It turned out that the issue wasn't with the strategy itself but with how we were communicating our message. We made subtle tweaks to the messaging, aligning it more closely with our audience's needs and expectations, and stayed the course. Over time, the campaign not only reached its targets but exceeded them, teaching me a valuable lesson about the rewards of resilience.

This experience shaped my approach to marketing strategy, instilling in me the belief that while innovation is vital, patience is equally important. It's about finding the balance between the two, ensuring that when you do make changes, they're the right ones—not just the expedient ones.

And learning this patience has paid off. I have a client that was a prospect for years before directly needing my marketing services to help with a new venture. Many people will tell you to remove such a prospect from your list, but if they are still reading my emails from time to time, still interacting with my social media from time to time, I believe in letting them remove themselves if and when they choose.

I helped him by creating a logo and developing a very basic website for his new venture, years after our first interaction. In fact, he was one of my very first clients after hanging my shingle, whom I had met from my prior corporate job. And now, a few years later, he's ready to spin-off that venture into one that is a bit more involved, and has reached out for a new and even more robust website.

Patience.

While anything online is ever-changing, the principles of patience and consistency remain steadfast. By embracing these values, you can ensure that your marketing efforts are not just flashes in the pan but enduring beacons of success.

Optimizing Campaign Duration

For all marketing campaigns, allowing time for the campaign to work is important. Even when it comes to discussing pay per click advertising on social media, such as Facebook advertising, entrepreneurs often grapple with the question of duration.

How long should a campaign run to be effective without overstaying its welcome or underperforming due to a premature finish? The answer is not straightforward, as it hinges on various factors, including the nature of the campaign, the audience's responsiveness, and the specific goals set by the business.

A Facebook ad campaign kicks off with a learning phase where the algorithm hones in on the most effective audience segments. This phase typically lasts a few days, during which the ad's performance may not be at its peak. Once the learning phase concludes, the ad first begins to reach what might be termed the 'low hanging fruit'—those users who are already familiar with your brand or have interacted with your page. This audience is more likely to engage with your content, making the initial period after the learning phase a critical time for gauging engagement levels.

If you tend to run your ads only a few days for each (such as "boosting" a post), you most likely are only ever reaching this low-hanging fruit of people who are *already* in your audience. (It's a bit different on Google and other platforms, but this tends to hold true for social PPC.)

However, the true test of a campaign's endurance lies in its ability to **extend beyond** this warm audience. After the initial burst of activity, you may notice a dip in engagement as the ad starts reaching a 'colder' audience—those who are less familiar with your brand. It's at this juncture that many might consider halting the campaign because the reach and engagement starts to decline from what you've seen the first few days, but patience is key. Continuing the campaign allows for repeated exposure, which is essential since the average person needs to encounter your message multiple times before they take action.

The duration of a campaign should also reflect the goal of expanding your audience (assuming that your goal isn't to reach only your current audience). If the objective is to introduce your brand to new prospects and increase awareness, a **longer campaign duration** is advisable. This extended period ensures that your message reaches individuals who require multiple interactions before they engage with your brand.

In determining the optimal duration for a campaign, it's crucial to strike a balance between giving the campaign enough time to perform and recognizing when it's time to refresh the creative elements. A campaign may run its course and require new visuals, copy, or offers to reinvigorate its ROI.

While there's no one-size-fits-all answer to the optimal campaign duration, a mix of short-term boosts and longer-running ads can be an effective strategy. It's essential to monitor the campaign's performance and be prepared to pivot when necessary. By understanding the nuances of your audience's engagement patterns and aligning your campaign duration with your marketing goals, you can optimize the impact of your digital advertising efforts.

It's clear that embracing digital marketing trends thoughtfully is crucial for entrepreneurs looking to stay competitive and relevant. From understanding the dynamic nature of marketing trends to leveraging AI, voice search, and video content, businesses must be agile and informed. The integration of AR and VR can create immersive experiences that simulate high-touch environments, while the strategic use of automation can enhance efficiency without sacrificing the personal touch.

As we look ahead, it's evident that the digital marketing landscape will continue to evolve, with current trends paving the way for new innovations. Entrepreneurs must not only keep pace with these changes but also anticipate and prepare for the future. By adopting a strategic approach to trend adoption, optimizing campaign durations, and learning from successful case studies, businesses can harness the power of digital marketing to achieve growth and maintain relevance in an ever-changing digital world.

Key Takeaways

- Understand the importance of patience and perseverance in marketing success.

- Embrace the 'Rule of 7' concept, acknowledging that consistent and repeated messaging is key to effective marketing.

- Develop a long-term marketing strategy that allows time for your message to resonate with your audience.

- Cultivate perseverance, recognizing that successful marketing often requires sustained effort and adaptation.

Beyond the Million Dollars: Long-Term Marketing Strategies

Setting the Stage for Sustained Growth

You've hit your initial financial targets – congratulations are in order! But don't let the popping corks distract you from the road ahead. The true test of entrepreneurial mettle isn't just in reaching milestones but in setting the stage for sustained growth. It's about shifting your mindset from short-term gains to long-term prosperity.

It's important to realize that the marketing strategies and business strategies that got you to where you are, usually are not the same ones that will get you to the next stage of where you want to go. While we have seen that entrepreneurs moving from four figures to figure figures, and five figures to six figures can employ a lot of the same strategies, moving from six figures to seven and beyond takes a different mindset and foundation.

Think of your business as a living entity; it evolves, adapts, and grows. Your marketing should do the same. This means setting progressive goals that not only match the pace of your business but also push its boundaries. It's not just about scaling up; it's about scaling smart. Your next steps should be as calculated as your first, with a clear vision that aligns with your evolving business landscape.

Marketing Mirror

What long-term marketing strategy have you implemented or plan to implement in your business?

_____

_____

How do you plan for and adapt your marketing strategies to align with your business growth and evolution?

_____

_____

Do you feel like your existing marketing mix is a strong foundation for long-term growth? Why or why not?

_____

_____

Principles of Scalable Marketing Strategies

Scalable marketing strategies are the backbone of sustained growth. They are the principles that ensure your marketing efforts grow in tandem with your business, without losing momentum or effectiveness. Here are the key principles to consider:

- **Flexibility:** The ability to pivot is crucial. Markets change, consumer behaviors shift, economics increase prices, and your marketing strategies need to be agile enough to adapt. This doesn't mean constant change but having the capacity to evolve your approach when necessary.
- **Data-Driven Decisions:** Your marketing should be guided by data, not guesswork. Use analytics to understand what works and what doesn't, and let these insights drive your strategy.
- **Customer-Centricity:** As your business grows, keep your focus on the customer. Scalable marketing strategies are built around deep customer understanding and the ability to meet their needs at every stage of your growth.
- **Consistent Branding:** While your tactics might change, your core brand message should remain steadfast. Consistency in branding ensures that as your reach expands, your identity remains recognizable and reliable. (This does not exclude making changes to finetune your brand voice; continue doing this until it's dialed in.)

- **Innovation:** Stay ahead of the curve by embracing new technologies and trends that can enhance your marketing efforts. This could mean leveraging AI for better customer insights or adopting new social media platforms to reach wider audiences.
- **Resource Allocation:** As you grow, so should your investment in marketing. This means not just financial resources but also investing in the right talent and tools to scale your efforts effectively.

By adhering to these principles, you're not just chasing the next big thing; you're building a marketing infrastructure that can support your business's growth for years to come. It's about laying a foundation that's robust yet flexible enough to support the weight of your ambitions and the dreams that drive them.

Case Study: Scaling Success

Background:

Let's examine the journey of a sustainable kitchenware company we will call EcoWare that started with a simple mission: to reduce plastic waste.

Initially, EcoWare's marketing strategy focused on raising awareness about plastic pollution and promoting their eco-friendly alternatives. They had a modest following, but the founders knew they had to scale their marketing efforts to match their ambition of becoming a market leader in sustainable home goods.

The Pivot:

EcoWare's first pivot came with the realization that their message needed to resonate on a more personal level. We helped them shift from a broad environmental message to one that showcased the direct impact customers could make with their purchases; the people, places and things and how they were impacted. This pivot was based on customer data and feedback, which highlighted the desire for tangible, individual contributions to sustainability.

Long-Term Strategies:

I worked with EcoWare began to implement several long-term marketing strategies:

Content Marketing Overhaul:
- Before: EcoWare's content was informative but lacked a personal touch.
- After: They started sharing customer stories, the journey of their products from conception to completion, and interactive content that allowed customers to see the difference they were making.

Community Building:
- Before: Engagement was primarily one-way, with EcoWare broadcasting messages to their audience.
- After: They fostered a community through social media groups, encouraging user-generated

content and discussions around sustainable living.

SEO and Voice Search Optimization:

- Before: EcoWare's online presence was not optimized for search engines or emerging technologies like voice search.
- After: They revamped their website with SEO best practices and optimized their content for voice search, making it easier for eco-conscious consumers to find them.

Utilizing AR for Product Previews:

- Before: Customers were hesitant to purchase without seeing the products in person.
- After: EcoWare introduced a VR option in their app where customers could drop right into some of the places that their purchases supported.

Customer Service AI Integration:

- Before: Customer inquiries were handled inconsistently, leading to varied customer experiences.
- After: They integrated a customer service AI that provided 24/7 support, learning from interactions to offer personalized assistance.

Challenges Overcome:

Scaling wasn't without its challenges. EcoWare faced issues with supply chain sustainability, ensuring their growing operations remained true to their eco-friendly ethos. They also had to navigate the balance between automation and personalization, particularly in customer service.

Lessons Learned:

Data is King: Every pivot and strategy was backed by customer data, ensuring decisions were customer-centric.

Adaptability is Crucial: The willingness to pivot and adapt strategies based on feedback and performance was key to their growth.

Consistency Maintains Trust: Despite the changes, EcoWare maintained a consistent brand message, which built trust and loyalty.

Technology Enhances Experience: The adoption of AR and AI didn't replace the human element; it enhanced the customer experience.

Universal Applications:

EcoWare's story is a testament to the power of strategic pivots and long-term planning. Their success illustrates that with the right approach, businesses can scale their marketing efforts to achieve and surpass their initial goals. The steps they took—listening to customers, leveraging technology, and remaining adaptable—are universal strategies that can be applied across industries.

Building a Marketing Ecosystem

The creation of a robust marketing ecosystem is paramount as a synergistic network where each marketing effort complements the others, creating a unified strategy that not only attracts customers but keeps them engaged and loyal.

Integration of Trends and Technologies:

To build this ecosystem, it's essential to integrate new marketing trends and technologies in a way that aligns with your core strategies. For instance, if voice search optimization is a trend you're adopting, ensure it's not just an add-on but a feature that enhances your existing content marketing efforts. Similarly, if you're exploring AI for customer service, it should be woven into your customer relationship management strategy to create a seamless experience.

Maintaining Core Strategies:

While it's tempting to chase every new trend, the key is to maintain a clear focus on your core strategies. These are the pillars of your marketing efforts that have proven effective. For example, if educational content has been a cornerstone of your marketing, any new tool or platform you use should support and amplify this content, not distract from it.

Marketing Mirror

Reflect on a time when you had to overhaul a marketing strategy. What prompted this change, and what was the outcome?

_____

_____

What lessons did you learn from this process that you can apply to future marketing strategies?

_____

_____

Innovation and Market Expansion

Innovation is the lifeblood of long-term marketing success. It's not just about new products or services; it's about innovating in how you market them and how you engage with your audience.

Strategies for Market Expansion:

Market expansion requires a keen eye for new opportunities and the courage to pursue them. This could mean targeting a new demographic, exploring untapped geographical markets, or even venturing into new digital spaces like emerging social media platforms.

Identifying Growth Opportunities:

To identify new opportunities, listen closely to your customers and analyze market trends. Use data-driven insights to determine where there's a demand for your products or services and where your marketing efforts can be most effective. For instance, if there's a growing interest in sustainable living, a company could capitalize on this trend by marketing their eco-friendly products to this burgeoning audience.

Building a marketing ecosystem and fostering innovation are not just strategies; they're commitments to the future of your business. By creating a marketing ecosystem, you ensure that every new trend or technology you adopt serves a purpose and contributes to a cohesive strategy. And through innovation, you keep your business at the forefront of market expansion and customer engagement.

As you move forward, remember that the integration of new trends should never overshadow the essence of what makes your brand unique. Keep your core strategies in sight and let them guide you as you explore new horizons. With a balance of innovation and consistency, your marketing efforts can support not just growth but a legacy of customer satisfaction and brand loyalty.

Key Takeaways

- Focus on developing long-term marketing strategies that drive sustainable growth.

- Look beyond short-term gains and aim for strategies that will build lasting success for your business.

- Continuously evaluate and adjust your marketing plan to align with changing market conditions and business objectives.

- Invest in building a strong brand and customer relationships that will pay dividends in the long run.

Conclusion

As we draw the curtains on this journey through the multifaceted landscape of marketing, it's time to reflect on the pivotal insights we've uncovered. From the initial understanding of the 'Rule of 7' to the strategic patience required for enduring success, each chapter has been a steppingstone towards a more profound marketing wisdom.

Recap of Key Messages:

We've delved into the essence of high-touch digital marketing, unraveling the psychological threads that bind customers to brands. We've navigated the ever-evolving realm of modern marketing trends, where AI, voice search, and video content are not just buzzwords but essential tools in your marketing arsenal. We've explored the importance of maintaining the human element in a digitized world, ensuring that technology enhances rather than replaces personal interaction.

We've also tackled the common missteps entrepreneurs make, pivoting towards actionable strategies that align with your business goals. Through case studies and personal anecdotes, we've illustrated the power of resilience, the rewards of consistency, and the significance of adopting a mindset geared towards sustained growth.

Call to Action:

Now, it's your turn to take these insights and translate them into action.

Remember, while this book provides the map, the journey is yours to embark upon. If you find yourself at a crossroads or in need of a compass to navigate the complex terrain of marketing, remember that professional guidance is just one conversation away.

Reach out to me for a 360° Marketing Assessment, where we'll take a holistic view of your marketing landscape. We can work together to identify your Zone of Genius, pivot away from the missteps, and stride confidently towards your milestones.

As you close this book, don't see it as the end, but as a launching pad for the next phase of your marketing journey. With the right strategies, a dash of innovation, and a partner to guide you, there's no limit to the success you can achieve.

Let's pivot together from missteps to milestones.

I can't wait to see how you succeed!

Appendix/Additional Resources

Resources

I would love to connect with you and be available as a resource for your marketing questions. Choose the connection that works best for you!

Need advice? Schedule a free 360° Marketing Assessment at my website - **https://vickywu.us/free-consultation**

Social Media

Facebook	facebook.com/vickywu.us
Instagram	@vickywuguru
Threads	@vickywuguru
X (Twitter)	@vickywuguru
LinkedIn	linkedin.com/company/vickywuguru
YouTube	@vickywuguru
WhatsApp	@vickywuguru

Podcast: "Your Marketing Department"

Audio	soundcloud.com/vickywuguru
Video	youtube.com/vickywuguru
Alexa	Say: "Alexa, play 'Your Marketing Department' on Apple Podcasts"

Or listen on your favorite podcast platform

Dictionary

Analytics:

The crystal ball of the digital age. Analytics give you a glimpse into the future by telling you what's worked in the past and what's happening right now.

B2C (Business to Consumer):

This is where you're talking directly to the everyday person, the end-user. It's about understanding and appealing to individual needs, desires, and emotions, making each consumer feel like your product or service was made just for them. Usually a relatively short sales cycle, sometimes with immediate purchases.

B2B (Business to Business):

Here, your audience is other businesses, usually with a fairly long sales cycle. It's a conversation between corporate entities, often centered around long-term solutions and partnerships. This audience usually has several layers of approvals; the person you're speaking to who is interested in your product usually is not the final approval, it may need to go through management, accounting and others.

B2P (Business to Professional):

When you're selling not just to businesses or consumers, but to the savvy entrepreneur. It's like having a conversation with someone who speaks your own secret business language. The sales process is usually somewhere between B2C and B2C.

Beyond-the-Graph Growth™:

This is a term I coined to help entrepreneurs think further than basic numbers. It isn't just about climbing the charts; it's about creating a symphony for your life. This helps entrepreneurs focus on strategies that aren't only about the bottom line, but that provide them with the lifestyle and freedom that they so desperately desire.

Bootstrapping:

Bootstrapping is like being the MacGyver of business finance. It's all about starting and growing your business using nothing but your own savings, sheer grit, and the cash flow from initial sales. Imagine launching a rocket with nothing but a slingshot and some serious elbow grease. That's bootstrapping. You're not relying on outside investors or hefty loans; instead, you're tightening your belt, getting creative with resources, and fueling your business dream with your own hard-earned cash.

CTA (Call to Action):

That little nudge or sometimes a full-on shove, urging your customers to take the leap from "Maybe I want this" to "Take my money!"

Fakexpert:

A portmanteau of 'fake' and 'expert', this term is reserved for those who talk the talk but couldn't walk the walk if they had a map and someone to carry them. They're often spotted sporting a library of buzzwords but lacking in the library of results.

Fractional CMO (Chief Marketing Officer):

Imagine having a marketing superhero on speed dial, ready to swoop in with a cape of experience and a toolkit of strategies, but only when you need them. That's a Fractional CMO for you! It's like renting a slice of a top-tier marketing brain, giving you access to years of wisdom, insights, and expertise, without the full-time executive price tag. Need a marketing mastermind for just an hour or two? No problem! A Fractional CMO is your go-to guru for big-picture thinking in bite-sized appointments. Perfect for when you want the brains without the full-time commitment. Opposite of Fakexpert.

Funnel:

An overused term to get you to part with your hard-earned dollar and buy "funnel software" that you may not need. It's billed as the magical pathway that creates sales. It's like a waterslide for customers – they hop in at the top, whoosh through your setup, and splash down into the pool of conversion. But if you ever sell anything, you already have some level of a funnel, even without software … it just may need some tuning.

KPI (Key Performance Indicator):

The scoreboard of the business world. These figures tell you if you're winning the game or if it's time to call a timeout and rethink your strategy.

Marketing MLM (Marketing Multi-Level Marketing):

We've all heard of MLMs but this isn't your grandma's Tupperware party. I use this term specifically for marketers who teach people their marketing system - the only system they know with only one way of doing things - and then those people have others pay to teach them the one system - and so on, and so on - and pretty soon 99% of the people offering "marketing" services are just selling this same one way to do it. They just slap their own name on it. We're not hobbits … there's more than one ring.

Niche

A niche is actually a small corner of a market where you are likely the only provider (or one of less than a handful). It's like finding that one spot in a crowded room where everyone is eager to hear what you have to say. While it might mean a smaller audience, it's packed with folks who are genuinely interested in your unique offerings. It's not just about being

a small fish; it's about being the big fish in a small, yet
perfectly formed pond!

Pivot (à la "Friends"):

Just like Ross, Chandler, and Rachel trying to maneuver a
couch up a staircase, sometimes you need to shift direction
to get where you're going. It's about finding a new angle
when the old one just won't fit through the door. You can
either get a smaller sofa, a bigger door, or pivot slightly.

ROI (Return on Investment):

The ultimate report card for your spending. It answers the
age-old question: "Did I make more money than I spent, or
is it time to go back to the drawing board?"

SEO (Search Engine Optimization):

The art of whispering sweet nothings into Google's ear so
that your website comes out playing hard to get... at the top
of the search results. Something that shouldn't be left to
beginners.

USP (Unique Service Proposition):

Your USP is like your business's secret sauce, that special
ingredient that makes your customers choose you over
anyone else. It's the superhero cape your brand wears,
making it stand out in a sea of sameness. Whether it's your
unmatched customer service, an innovative product feature,
or a unique pricing structure, your USP is what makes your

business not just a choice, but *the* choice. It's your business's fingerprint, unique and identifying, leaving a memorable impression on your customers.

Zone of Genius:

That sweet spot where your skills and passions collide, creating an explosion of productivity and satisfaction. It's the business equivalent of hitting every green light on your way to work. The portion of your business that only you can do.

Other common terms you probably already know from the book (these aren't alphabetical but in an order that makes sense with each other):

Content Marketing:

The art of selling without selling. It's about wooing your customers with words and wisdom until they can't help but fall for your brand.

Lead Magnet:

The digital equivalent of "free samples." It's a tasty morsel of content that lures potential customers into your funnel.

Engagement:

Not the diamond-ring kind, but just as valuable. It's the measure of how much your audience interacts with your brand, and it's pure gold in the marketing world.

Brand Equity:

The love (and value) people have for your brand. It's what makes customers choose you over the generic option, every time.

Customer Persona:

Your ideal customer, brought to life. It's like creating a character for a novel, except this character is the star of your marketing strategies.

Engagement Rate:

Think of it as the applause meter at a rock concert. It's not just about how many tickets you sell (followers you have), but how many fans are screaming your name (interacting with your content). But unlike a rock concert where ticket sales = revenue, engagement alone isn't enough. Rock on with relevance!

Vanity Metrics:

These are the high heels of data: they might give your stats a lift and look fabulous, but they won't help you run a marathon. Remember, it's not just about height; it's about going the distance with meaningful metrics (such as profit).

Conversion Rate:

This is the alchemy of marketing, turning casual browsers into golden customers. It's less about casting a wide net and more about crafting the perfect spell to charm the right ones into your cauldron of clients.

Customer Loyalty:

The secret ingredient in your marketing gumbo. It's what keeps customers coming back for seconds, thirds, and even bringing friends to the table. It's not just about the first taste; it's about creating a flavor they can't forget.

Sunk Cost Fallacy:

The stubborn cousin of investment, where you keep throwing darts even after realizing the dartboard is on the other wall. It's continuing to eat a bad pizza because you already paid for it. Now you either have a wall full of dart holes or food poisoning.

Revenue:

Imagine your business as a bustling marketplace. Revenue is the total cash your stalls rake in, from the shiny trinkets to the big-ticket items. It's the bustling crowd of sales, the jingle in your pocket from every transaction. But remember, it's not just about how much you sell; it's about what you keep after the market closes.

Revenue Growth:

The grand finale of your marketing fireworks show. If your strategies aren't lighting up the sky and making the crowd go 'ooh' and 'aah' with sales, it's time to rework your display.

Profit:

This is the treasure chest at the end of your entrepreneurial adventure. It's what's left after your ship braves the stormy seas of expenses. Think of profit as the true north on your business compass – guiding you towards financial success. It's not just about the size of the bounty; it's about how much you can sail home with after battling the expenses beast. Profit beats revenue every time.

Action Plan:

Your Post-Book Roadmap to Marketing Mastery

Audit Your Current Marketing Efforts:

- Review your current marketing strategies and assess what's working and what's not.
- Use the 360° Marketing Assessment approach to get a holistic view.

Identify Your Zone of Genius:

- Pinpoint the areas where you excel and can make the most impact.
- Delegate or outsource tasks that don't fall within this zone.

Define Your Business Goals:

- Set clear, measurable objectives for what you want to achieve with your marketing.
- Ensure these goals align with your overall business strategy.

Understand Your Audience:

- Create detailed customer personas to better target your marketing efforts.

- Consider conducting surveys or interviews to gather more insights.

Refine Your Brand Messaging:

- Ensure your brand message is clear, consistent, and compelling across all channels.
- Use the 'Rule of 7' to reinforce your message through repeated exposure.

Embrace Modern Marketing Trends:

- Evaluate which digital marketing trends can benefit your business.
- Start small with one or two trends to avoid becoming overwhelmed.

Optimize for Voice and Video:

- Adjust your content strategy to include voice search optimization.
- Incorporate video content to engage and retain customer attention.

Leverage AI and Automation:

- Implement AI tools like chatbots to enhance customer service.
- Use automation to streamline repetitive tasks without losing the personal touch.

Develop a Content Strategy:

- Plan a content calendar that aligns with your marketing goals and customer needs.
- Use storytelling to create an emotional connection with your audience.

Implement High-Touch Marketing Tactics:

- Integrate sensory marketing elements to evoke emotions and memories.
- Maintain the human element in your digital interactions.

Monitor and Analyze Your Results:

- Regularly check your analytics to understand the effectiveness of your strategies.
- Adjust your tactics based on data-driven insights.

Practice Strategic Patience:

- Give your strategies time to work; don't pivot too quickly.
- Be resilient and learn from both successes and missteps.

Plan for Scalability:

- Develop marketing strategies that can grow with your business.

- Stay flexible and be ready to adapt to changing market conditions.

Seek Continuous Improvement:

- Always look for ways to innovate and improve your marketing efforts.
- Stay curious and open to new ideas and approaches.

Reach Out for Professional Guidance:

- If you're feeling overwhelmed or unsure, consider reaching out for a Beyond-the-Graph Growth™ consultation.
- Use professional services to refine your strategies and accelerate your growth.

Remember, this action plan is a starting point. Your journey to marketing mastery is unique, and you'll need to tailor these steps to fit your business's specific needs and goals. Keep learning, keep testing, and keep growing!

About the Author

With a marketing career spanning over three decades, Vicky Wu stands at the forefront of marketing innovation, blending time-tested strategies with innovative tactics to drive business growth and revenue. As a Fractional CMO, Vicky doesn't just walk the talk—she coaches entrepreneurs to run the marathon, applying her extensive expertise to foster the expansion of businesses ranging from startups to Fortune 500 companies.

Vicky's marketing philosophy is simple yet profound: your business isn't cookie cutter, and your marketing shouldn't be either. She excels in customizing strategies that resonate with a company's unique DNA, ensuring that each marketing plan not only aligns with the business's values and objectives but also appropriately fits their budget. A specialty is helping entrepreneurs overcome marketing missteps that may have been made, and help others set things up right from the start.

Her approach is about translating the 'big league' tactics from those huge guys with really deep pockets, into actionable, cost-effective plans for small and medium-sized businesses.

Her journey in marketing began with the whimsical creation of amusement parks on paper as a young artist, a venture that unknowingly laid the foundation for her branding acumen, followed by an early start in a marketing career and a degree in Business and Marketing. Today, Vicky's creative canvas is much larger, yet her passion for helping businesses succeed remains the driving force behind her work. She has crafted a suite of best practices that deliver exceptional Return on Investment, regardless of the industry or company size.

Vicky's commitment extends beyond the corporate sphere. She is passionate about giving back, supporting eco-friendly initiatives, and empowering minority and women-owned businesses. Quarterly she gives back to the community through pro-bono support of a nonprofit or a deserving bootstrapped entrepreneur. Her work is her way of making a positive impact on the world, one marketing strategy at a time.

Vicky likes to take the marketing strategies that she learned—and created—at Fortune 500 companies and multi-million- and multi-billion-dollar organizations and bring that level of experience to entrepreneurs who wouldn't otherwise have access to the same level of expertise as those big guys and their deep pockets with seemingly limitless resources.

www.ingramcontent.com/pod-product-compliance
Lightning Source LLC
Chambersburg PA
CBHW071539210326
41597CB00019B/3055